Pathway of
PEACE

Cindy,
God bless you
and keep you in His peace.
Cheryl E

October,

De blev vor ...

one happy vor de his point.

Cheers?

Pathway of PEACE

Living in a Growing Relationship with Christ

Discussion Questions
Available at
www.cherylelton.com

Cheryl Elton

MOUNTAINTOP PRESS

Pathway of Peace: Living in a Growing Relationship with Christ
Copyright © 2014 by Cheryl Elton

ISBN 978-0-9903361-0-5

Library of Congress Control Number: 2014907670

Published by Mountaintop Press
Queensbury, NY 12804

Cover design by: Matthew Elton and Tim Cox Jr.

Printed in the United States of America

CONTENTS

Author's Note

I'm a list person. To-do lists, shopping lists, record-keeping lists. Almost anything you can think of, I have a list for. As I work through my daily tasks, there's something fulfilling about ticking things off the list one by one. If I do something major not on my list, I'll actually write it in just for the shameless satisfaction of then crossing it off. Maybe this sounds crazy, but if you're also a list person you are probably smiling right now.

I've been this way my whole life. I learned it from my mother, who was extremely practical and organized. A dedicated homemaker, she took down all the curtains in the house, washed, ironed, and put them back up not once, but twice a year. Her kitchen floor was always clean. My mother kept meticulous records on everything, from car insurance payments to when the furnace was last serviced. When she and my dad purchased a new appliance, the catalog was dated with the receipt neatly stapled to the cover, then filed away. Everything had its place and was in its place. I'll admit my home today wouldn't quite pass mother's white glove test, but I am equally well organized.

From this upbringing grew my own love affair with lists. For me, writing things down keeps my thoughts and my life organized. I'm more settled because I know what needs to be done. I also like to make goals, and have done so since the age of fourteen when I became a Christian.

My freshman year in high school a few friends enthusiastically began sharing Scriptures with me from a Bible class they were taking. I was both surprised and excited to learn something about God that not only seemed to make sense, but also was simple.

One day my friend Cindy shared with me a verse from the gospel of Mark that says whatever I ask for in prayer I will receive, if I only believe.[1]

"Could it really be this simple?" I thought. "All I need do is ask and believe?"

In all my years attending Sunday school I remembered learning that I *should* pray, but never really *how* to pray.

"Can I really talk to God any time?" I wondered. "Why would He be that interested in *me*?"

As a child I was extremely shy and afraid of interacting with people. My parents were not socialites and rarely did we have guests in our home. When the peer pressures of youth came, I had little self-assurance. But when I learned from the Scriptures that I am wonderfully and awesomely made, precious and beautiful in the sight of God, it no longer mattered what others thought of me! My confidence soared. God loved me, what else did I need? My heart was filled with joy. For the first time life had meaning. I longed to make God's purposes my own. Thus began my lifelong quest into understanding the Word of God and developing my relationship with Him.

On a hot August day when I was twenty years old, I sat quietly praying with pen and paper in hand. I was making my annual "goals" list. On that list were many things you'd expect from a young adult. Things like *finish college, get married, have a family,* and (I laugh to think it now) *someday* (when I'm really old—like in my forties!)—*write a book.*

Then it came to me—how cool would it be to set a "lifetime goal"? What would that even look like? What is the one thing I really want my entire life to be about?

Surely a spiritual goal would be better than *making a lot of money,* or *being successful in my career,* or even *being a good parent.* So I thought of things like *being a more loving person,* or *sharing the gospel more.*

As I continued to think, I realized what I really want for my whole life is to do what God wants me to do. For that, I need to be able to hear His voice. To do that, I need to be peaceful inside and not doubt Him.

So my lifetime goal became: **To be at perfect peace in my heart all the time.**

I chose as my theme verse Isaiah 26:3:

You will keep in perfect peace all who trust in you, all whose thoughts are fixed on you!

Now, I'll be honest in telling you that over the years there have been periods of time when I've lost focus of that goal. I've allowed myself to get swallowed up by circumstances. At times my anxious thoughts have led me to make decisions I'd later regret. I've often worried, instead of giving my cares to God and trusting Him.

But again and again I have seen the Lord's patient and gracious hand upon my life. Through the peaks and valleys of life—the heartaches, disappointments, and chaos, as well as the joys and triumphs—I have repeatedly found my way back to the peacefulness of His presence. The Lord has never left me.

Today, I am closer in my relationship with Him than I was a year ago. And God willing, I hope to be even closer to Him by this time next year. I'm striving to seek His presence more consistently. I am learning to walk in His peace and hear His voice.

How about you? Do you yearn for more inner peace? Do you long to hear the Lord's voice more? Have you learned to thirst for His presence and find your rest and refreshment from the fountain of living waters, Jesus Christ?

It's my desire that this book will help lead you to all of these.

Jesus Christ *is* the Prince of Peace. My prayer is that as we journey together through these pages you will find inspiration to grow in relationship with Him, deepen your faith, learn to hear His voice, and come to experience His perfect peace greater than ever before.

For it's in His presence alone, we find peace.

Cheryl A. Elton

Part One

The Highest Perfection

To need God is man's highest perfection.
~Soren Kierkegaard[1]

CHAPTER 1

Our Deepest Need

There I sat at what I was sure was the world's longest red light. As I waited, I felt the familiar wave of indigestion pass through my stomach. I swallowed hard to push back the burning in my throat. My doctor's visit had run longer than expected, and I was now running late to pick up my five-year-old son from school. My other son, age two, was growing restless in his car seat in the back.

"Will this light ever change?" I wondered, as the seconds passed like glaciers. My mind was already picturing my kindergartener standing outside the school in tears, wondering why I wasn't there for him.

In my purse was a script for my latest medication. Oh yes—I needed to stop at the pharmacy to fill it and then run into the grocery store for the few things I'd forgotten to get for dinner. Inwardly, I was already dreading getting home and trying to cook with the two boys going at each other's throats. They had recently reached that wonderful age where they were starting to aggravate each other. As the younger one grabbed one of the older one's toys, their voices would rise in a cacophony of cries pleading *"Mom! Do something!"*

In the past two months I'd been to the doctor three times and this would be the fourth medication to try to help settle my stomach, which hurt almost all the time. I'd been diagnosed with irritable bowel syndrome and now, acid reflux. Hopefully this one would help.

So far, nothing had . . .

———————<☞>———————

Sadly, situations like this are all too common, even for those who acknowledge God's presence in their lives. When challenging or stressful circumstances persist, it is all too easy to become swallowed up by them and lose our focus.

It's estimated that 75-90% of all doctor visits in the United States are for stress-induced illnesses. Anxiety and the trauma of stress can play a major part in physical conditions such as headaches, high blood pressure, heart conditions, diabetes, skin disorders, asthma, arthritis, and stomach ailments. At one time, the U.S. government declared stress a hazard of the workplace. In fact, it costs American industry more than $300 billion annually in missed work and related health care.[1]

As life presses in on us from every direction, stress-related sicknesses continue to grow exponentially around the world. New drugs are invented every year to treat anxiety and the countless symptoms of its associated ailments.

As millions of people search in vain for that elusive peace of mind to calm their troubled nerves, Jesus' words in John 14:27 still speak truth:

*I am leaving you with **a gift—peace of mind and heart**. And the peace I give is a gift the world cannot give. So don't be troubled or afraid.*

Our Deepest Need

Christ has given us the gift of peace! So why are we not always peaceful? How do we grab hold of this peace and allow it to rule our hearts and minds? As the world and life's endless demands continuously barrage us, is it possible to really live with this peace each day?

The God-Shaped Hole

Give a dog a bone to chew and a warm fireplace to curl up beside, and it will be totally content. Give a cat a scratching post and a sunny windowsill, and it will be entirely satisfied. But give a man or woman everything he or she could ever want, and they eventually grow restless, remain unsatisfied.

Unlike animals, people desire meaning and purpose in life. We are all born with physical, mental, emotional, and spiritual needs that long to be met. We all desire to love and be loved. Aren't most of our lives spent in pursuit of love, happiness, meaning, and peace?

The world continually takes advantage of our restlessness. We're bombarded with advertisements and the media telling us if we only buy this product . . . if we only were more attractive . . . if we only take this class . . . if we only read this book . . . if we only make more money . . . *then* we will find peace and fulfillment in life. And sad to say, many of us have unknowingly bought into these falsehoods.

Most people follow the world's way—spending their lives pursuing money, education, and material possessions, often while bouncing from relationship to relationship in search of love and self-esteem. Some people become so driven that they work multiple jobs in an effort to make more money—even if it means sacrificing time with their families. Eventually exhausted, stressed out, and burdened down with all their "stuff," their health often deteriorates. At long last they retire thinking, "Finally, I will have relaxation and peace." But having never invested themselves in anything of lasting value, never having spent enough time with their loved ones, and not knowing what to do with all the money they've made, they still feel empty.

This scenario is not unusual.

The book of Ecclesiastes tells us *"History merely repeats itself. It has all been done before. Nothing under the sun is truly new."*[2]

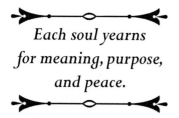

Each soul yearns for meaning, purpose, and peace.

King Solomon tried it all. Searching for meaning and fulfillment in life, he pursued every pleasure, amassing great wealth for himself, building huge gardens and parks, and marrying 700 wives. To this day, the Pools of Solomon—an impressive collection of ancient swimming pools believed to have been built by the King himself—stand three miles southwest of Bethlehem.

Solomon seemingly had it all—wealth, women, and political power—yet nothing ultimately satisfied his desire for meaning in life. In the end, his conclusion was:

"Everything is meaningless," says the Teacher, "completely meaningless! I observed everything going on under the sun, and really, it is all meaningless—like chasing the wind." (Ecclesiastes 1:2, 14)

The Dalai Lama put it this way:

Man sacrifices his health in order to make money. Then he sacrifices money to recuperate his health. And then he is so anxious about the future that he does not enjoy the present; the result being that he does not live in the present or the future; he lives as if he is never going to die, and then dies having never really lived.

Many of the world's wealthiest people are also the most health-deprived and depressed. C.S. Lewis wrote that every man and woman has within them a "God-shaped hole." We try to fill it with many things, but always come up short. Only our loving Creator can fill the void.

The Most Important Relationship

Deep within the heart of every person is a longing to know the Creator. Every man and woman has the desire and need for "someone" to be in control of the unknown. Each soul yearns for meaning, purpose, and peace.

The New Testament book of James speaks of the brevity of our lives:

Look here, you who say, "Today or tomorrow we are going to a certain town and will stay there a year. We will do business there and make a profit." How do you know what your life will be like tomorrow? Your life is like the morning fog—it's here a little while, then it's gone. What you ought to say is, "If the Lord wants us to, we will live and do this or that." (James 4:13-16)

None of us knows what tomorrow will bring. We only have today to live. Daily we choose: will I live for myself or for God? Will I follow my ways or His?

If you knew your end was near, what might you be thinking about? Would it be how much money you have in the bank, or your occupation? Would it be the opportunities you had—or missed?

In life's final moments, what often matters most is the important people in our lives—those we love or who love us. It's not uncommon for a dying person to "hang in there" until family members or other loved ones come to say goodbye. Why? Because the people they love are their most valued treasure.

When we strip away all the activities and all the façades, life is about relationships—with others and with God. Yet, how often we take for granted those relationships that mean the most: our spouse, our children, our parents, and our friends— the people we see and speak with. When it comes to an invisible God, how much easier it becomes to neglect our relationship with Him, to take it for granted, or to even forget Him.

From the beginning of time, God wanted a family. He created man and woman so that He could share intimate relationship with His children. Yet many people, including Christians, are confused about how to develop such a relationship. How do you get close to an invisible God? How do you hold a conversation with someone who doesn't, at first, seem to talk back?

God Devised a Solution

Any close or cherished relationship requires sharing and communication, and our Creator has lovingly revealed His heart in the pages of the Bible, His written words to us. It tells us of a God who is loving, kind, full of mercy and judgment. It reveals the sorry state we are all born into, separated from God through our evil and sinful thoughts and actions. With the fall of humankind in the Garden of Eden,[3] our spiritual connection with God was severed. We are born strangers to God's way of thinking, no longer at peace with Him as He originally intended.[4]

Jesus Christ—the grand subject of the Bible—is God's purpose of the ages. Only through belief in Him are we made right with God, that we may freely enter His presence. The book of Colossians tells us we are brought into God's presence through the death of Jesus Christ.

> *Yet now he has reconciled you to himself through the death of Christ in his physical body. As a result, he has brought you into his own presence . . . (Colossians 1:22a)*

God, in His loving-kindness, offers the free gift of salvation to all who believe.

> *If you confess with your mouth that Jesus is Lord and believe in your heart that God raised him from the dead, you will be saved. For it is by believing in your heart that you are made right with God, and it is by confessing with your mouth that you are saved. (Romans 10:9-10)*

This salvation is so magnificent it can never be earned. It is a gift, freely given by God's grace.[5] Only by His goodness are we freed from the power of sin.[6] Even those who live a "good" life need to be brought into a peaceful relationship with God. We are created for His glory, and only through intimate relationship with God through Jesus Christ is this restless hunger satisfied.

In the words of Augustine, *"Thou has made us for thyself, O Lord, and our heart is restless until it finds its rest in thee."*[7]

CHAPTER 2

The Many Faces of Peace

When you think of the word "peace," what comes to mind? A sunset by the lake on a warm summer's night? A snowy afternoon spent in your easy chair by the fire with a good book and a cup of tea? The kids being out of the house for a few hours? Peace comes in many shapes, sizes, and shades of meaning. Sometimes we feel life is peaceful just by the absence of negative or stressful circumstances. We say we're more "at peace" simply by being less busy. Having money in the bank or a good doctor's report gives us "peace of mind." Let's take a look at the various ways the dictionary defines **peace:**

- **Freedom from disturbance; tranquility.** *He just wanted to have dinner in peace.*
- **Mental calm; serenity.** *The peace of mind this insurance gives you . . .*
- **Freedom from or the cessation of war or violence.** *The Straits were to be open to warships in time of peace.*

There are common phrases we use when we talk about **being at peace:**

- **Free from anxiety or stress.** *He finally felt at peace about going on the trip.*
- **Dead and therefore free from the difficulties of life.** *She's finally at peace.*
- **In a state of friendliness.** *There's a man at peace with the world.*

At times a person may **hold one's peace:**
- **Remain silent about something.** *He nodded indulgently but held his peace.*

We **keep the peace:**
- **Refrain or prevent others from disturbing civil order.** *The police officer tried to get the students to keep the peace.*

Or we **make peace:**
- **Re-establish friendly relations.** *She returned home to make peace with her brother.*[1]

Peace is Undisturbed Faith

For the Christian, peace is a deep spiritual reality we receive at the time of the new birth in Christ. When that God-shaped hole becomes filled through faith in Christ, we are "made right" with God—once again at peace with Him.

*Therefore, since we have been made right in God's sight by faith, **we have peace with God** because of what Jesus Christ our Lord has done for us. (Romans 5:1)*

The peace Christ gives us is not the kind of peace that the world or anything in it can offer. Our minds cannot fully comprehend this peace, but our hearts can sense its presence.

> Then **you will experience God's peace,** which exceeds anything we can understand. His peace will guard your hearts and minds as you live in Christ Jesus. (Philippians 4:7)

The peace of Christ is so magnificent, so unique, that God Himself says it *"exceeds anything we can understand."*

In *Sparkling Gems from the Greek,* author Rick Renner further defines this peace:

> The word "peace" comes from the Greek word **eirene,** the Greek equivalent for the Hebrew word **shalom,** which expresses the idea of **wholeness, completeness, or tranquility in the soul that is unaffected by the outward circumstances or pressures.** The word *eirene* strongly suggests the rule of order in place of chaos.

> When a person is dominated by peace, he has a calm, inner stability that results in the ability to conduct himself peacefully, even in the midst of circumstances that would normally be very nerve-wracking, traumatic, or upsetting . . . Rather than allowing the difficulties and pressures of life to break him, a person who is possessed by peace is **whole, complete, orderly, stable, and poised for blessing.**[2]

The peace of God has no strife or trouble in it. It is undisturbed faith in Him.

Peace is Full Awareness of His Presence

Jesus puts a face on God. We relate to His humanity.

Jesus Christ, the Son of God, walked the earth as a man. He wasn't born into wealth, status, or prestige. From His humble beginning, born in a manger, He was cared for by His parents. As a child He learned and grew.[3]

Scripture tells us Jesus struggled with the things of this life and was tested in every way we are, yet did not yield to temptation or sin. Jesus showed emotions. He cried when His friend Lazarus died. He showed concern to a hungry crowd. He got angry at injustice. Surely, He understands our struggles and temptations, as well as our joys.

This High Priest of ours understands our weaknesses, for he faced all of the same testings we do, yet he did not sin. (Hebrews 4:15)

As you read the gospel records you see Jesus' undying compassion, love, and mercy for all people. The woman caught in adultery. The many who came to Him for healing. His entire life portrayed the love and presence of an awesome God.

*For a child is born to us, a son is given to us. The government will rest on his shoulders. And he will be called: Wonderful Counselor, Mighty God, Everlasting Father, **Prince of Peace**. (Isaiah 9:6)*

Jesus Christ is called the "Prince of Peace." Might this name have to do with His spiritual connection to the Father? In order to lead a sinless life and perfectly carry out God's will, Christ had to be in close relationship with the Father, hearing and obeying His voice, walking in His peace.

Through Christ, we too live in God's presence, experience His peace, and learn to hear His voice. Jesus wants each of us to know Him personally, not simply as a historical figure or someone we read about, but as Lord, master, and friend. To live in God's peace requires a continuous acknowledgment, attentiveness, and awareness of His presence.

He tells us *"I will never leave you nor forsake you"*[4]—yet how often do we leave Him?

In the busyness of our lives we must develop the art of being quiet within, resting our hearts in that secret place of God's presence. As we do so, it becomes easier to access Him any time throughout the day, for " . . . *those who seek me diligently will find me."*[5]

> *Peace in Christ is a full awareness of His presence, no matter the circumstance.*

As Christians, we can get off the world's interminable treadmill and learn to be at peace in Him regardless of our circumstances. In Christ alone we are overcomers:

*I have told you this so that **you may have peace in me.** Here on earth you will have many trials and sorrows. But take heart, because **I have overcome the world.** (John 16:33).*

But you belong to God, my dear children. You have already won a victory over those people, because the Spirit who lives in you is greater than the spirit who lives in the world. (1 John 4:4)

Peace in Christ is a full awareness of His presence, no matter the circumstance. It is not like anything the world offers. Once you have tasted it, you will yearn more and more for the rest that is found in Him.

Draw close to Him to experience it. Ask Him to lead you in His ways. Talk to Him often throughout the day, and share your life with Him. Jesus Christ craves your most intimate fellowship. Moment by moment seek Him with a humble heart, acknowledging that His thoughts are higher than yours, and His ways are not your ways.

Seek to share conversation, closeness, and camaraderie with Him, so that it becomes characteristic of your days. The Lord will reward you with more of Himself, as you dwell in His peaceful presence.

CHAPTER 3

Are You a Hebrew or a Greek?

October 17, 2016. December 21, 2012. These are predicted dates for Jesus Christ's second coming, and the end of the world. The book *88 Reasons Why the Rapture Will be in 1988* by Edgar Whisenant sold more than 4.5 million copies. At the time he was quoted as saying, "Only if the Bible is in error am I wrong; and I say that to every preacher in town." His predicted dates of September 11-13, 1988 came and went. Whisenant continued to make predictions and write books about Christ's return until 1997, but gained less and less attention with each failed date.

History is replete with those who have set a date for the Lord's return—only to watch those dates come and go. Many Christians today become immersed in studying end-time events in the Scriptures. Maybe you have. It's common to lay out all these events on a timeline with exact dates, and even times of various occurrences. This kind of thinking is typical to those of us living in the western world. Our concept of time—points on a line—is of little concern, however, to the Hebrew mind. Since the Bible has Hebraic roots, understanding it and approaching it with a Hebrew mindset can help give us great insight into its truths.

Most of us born in the western world unknowingly view the Scriptures through our western thinking, which was influenced by Greek philosophy. The emphasis of biblical Judaism is quite different. The main difference is between *knowing* and *doing*. The Greek exalts knowledge and right thinking, while the Hebrew is more concerned with right living, practice, and relationship.

Intellectually most of us are Greeks, not Hebrews. In our quest to study the Bible, we find we don't want to live with any apparent contradiction, inconsistency, or difficult-to-explain passage. We like everything to be in logical, systematic patterns, organized in tight, carefully reasoned theologies. We like keys and formulas.

The western mindset says it's more important to believe "the right thing" than to live the right way. This emphasis on "getting the right doctrine" helps explain why we have so many denominations today, and why many are so focused on what one believes that it's sometimes at the expense of godly living and the unity God desires among Christians.

> *The Hebrews sought the things of God, not in an effort to comprehend everything, but in order to revere Him more greatly.*

Biblical Jews, with their inherently eastern mindset, viewed the supernatural as affecting everything. They emphasized relationship with God and others over laws of science and the material. The Hebrew mindset extols behavior and godly living as the substance and meaning of life. The Hebrews sought the things of God, not in an effort to comprehend everything, but in order to revere Him more greatly. This is dramatically significant.

If you were to ask someone with Greek thinking how they would define God, you might hear something like: Creator, Spirit, the Almighty One, Supreme Being, Omniscient (all-knowing), Omnipotent (all-powerful), or Omnipresent (everywhere-present). All of these would be true. The Hebrew response, however, might be something like: God is my rock, my strength, my peace, my healer, my deliverer, my shepherd, the fountain of living waters—emphasizing His relational aspects.

Instead of describing God using attributes of accomplishment, the eastern mind describes Him by how He relates to them. It would be similar to describing your uncle merely by saying he is a famous lawyer versus your relative.

In our example of end-time events, the sequential order in which God will do things is of little concern to the Hebrew—rather the focus is primarily on the promise that He *will* act.

For most of us westerners, the Hebrew mindset is so foreign to us that we easily fall into the comfort of our Greek thinking when reading the Bible. We become obsessed with doctrinal statements, creeds, and definitions, and the quest to systematically figure out every point of doctrine. Even the Godhead must be tightly defined and structured. This thinking is thoroughly western and Greek.

In contrast, the Hebrews accepted the idea that some things about God are a "mystery." In the Hebraic view, relationship with Jesus Christ is more important than defining Him. Do we really know Him as Lord? Do we walk and talk with Him daily?

Today we see much "technique-oriented" Christianity. We love practices we can apply to get into, or out of, situations. We love "keys" for living the abundant life, and seek techniques for financial prosperity, inner healing, and receiving spiritual power.

In the book *God in Search of Man*, Jewish theologian Abraham Heschel writes:

> *The Greeks learned in order to comprehend. The Hebrews learned in order to revere. The modern man learns in order to use.*[1]

In the days when Jesus' Kingdom movement was called the "sect of the Nazarenes" (Acts 24:5,14), being a Christian was about relationship with God through Jesus Christ and relationship with one's fellow man. Since that time, the church has greatly de-emphasized relationship with God and Christ, and instead intellectualized and commercialized the faith.

Finding Greater Meaning

To deepen our understanding of what it means to be a follower of Christ and to develop our relationship with Him, perhaps it would do us all good to return to the roots of our faith and think more like the Hebrews. I encourage you to keep this in mind as we continue exploring peace in Christ.

In the upcoming chapters I'll also occasionally discuss the meaning of a word from its original Greek (New Testament) or Hebrew (Old Testament) translation. If you've never done this, don't feel intimidated. It's not difficult or technical. Rather, I trust that you too will find it thrilling to understand some of the deeper nuances of words and how they enrich our understanding of a passage of Scripture.

CHAPTER 4

Wisdom From Forrest

One of my favorite movies is the 1994 blockbuster *Forrest Gump*.[1] It's the story of a mentally challenged man's epic journey through life, influencing popular culture and experiencing first-hand major events in American history between the 1950s and the 1980s. Forrest's story is a beautiful balance between laughter and melancholy, rich in quiet truths that touch the heart.

With Forrest's IQ of 75, one could easily think he doesn't understand much of what happens to him. In reality, he understands everything he needs to know, and the rest, the story suggests, is excess. He knows what is important about love and remains faithful to his first love, Jenny, throughout his life— even though she tells him "Forrest, you don't know what love is," as she spends years trying to find herself.

Forrest is a dignified, no-nonsense man, and we come to admire his incredible integrity and simplicity toward life. Although he appears stupid, we see from his actions he is far from it. A famous line from the movie is "Stupid is as stupid does"—perhaps a modern way to represent what Jesus said: *"You can identify them by their fruit, that is, by the way they act."*[2]

Doers, Not Just Listeners

Jesus says that those who love Him are they who accept and obey His words.[3]

The simple truth is that if we love God above all else we will demonstrate it by obedience to His commandments.

We know we love God's children if we love God and obey his commandments. Loving God means keeping his commandments, and his commandments are not burdensome. (1 John 5:2-3)

But don't just listen to God's word. You must do what it says. Otherwise, you are only fooling yourselves. (James 1:22)

Holman's Illustrated Bible Dictionary says biblical obedience is "to hear God's Word and act accordingly." Many people can quote the Bible. Many read it regularly. Yet if we aren't doing what it says, what's the point? It makes no tangible difference in the way we live. This truth comes to life in a story from the book *Living Above the Level of Mediocrity* by Charles Swindoll. He writes:

Imagine, if you will, that you work for a company whose president found it necessary to travel out of the country and spend an extended period of time abroad. So he says to you and the other trusted employees, "Look, I'm going to leave. And while I'm gone, I want you to pay close attention to the business. You manage things while I'm away. I will write you regularly. When I do, I will instruct you in what you should do from now until I return from this trip."

Everyone agrees. He leaves and stays gone for a couple of years. During that time he writes often, communicating his desires and concerns. Finally he returns. He walks up to the front door of the company and immediately discovers everything is in a mess—weeds flourishing in the flower beds, windows broken across the front of the building, the gal at the front desk dozing, loud music roaring from several offices, two or three people engaged in horseplay in the back room. Instead of making a profit, the business has suffered a great loss. Without hesitation he calls everyone together and with a frown asks, "What happened? Didn't you get my letters?" You say, "Oh, yeah, sure. We got all your letters. We've even bound them in a book. And some of us have memorized them. In fact, we have a 'letter study' every Sunday. You know, those were really great letters."

I think the president would then ask, "But what did you do about my instructions?" And, no doubt the employees would respond, "Do? Well, nothing. But we read every one!"[4]

We can guess what would probably happen after this. The next day there would be a lot more people on line at the unemployment office. The employees would be fired for insubordination—not doing what they were responsible for. Many people go to church on Sunday. Many read the Bible. We can memorize it, quote it, study it regularly, hang framed verses in our kitchens, and even share it with others, yet easily choose not to practice it and be obedient to it in our everyday lives.

Those who spend time reading and meditating upon the Scriptures learn God's heart—His will for their lives. He promises to multiply grace and peace to us through the knowledge of Him.

> *May God give you **more and more** grace and **peace** as you grow in your knowledge of God and Jesus our Lord.*
> *(2 Peter 1:2)*

God promises peace to those who love His words. Christians should love the Word of God more than any of the world's finest riches.

> *Those who love your instructions **have great peace** and do not stumble. (Psalm 119:165)*

> *Truly, I love your commands more than gold, even the finest gold. (Psalm 119:127)*

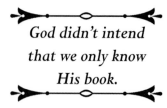

God didn't intend that we only know His book.

We should come to the Word of God with great joy and respect. For in addition to instructing us in God's ways, it helps us grow into an active relationship with Jesus Christ as a living being. God speaks to us through His written Word. He also speaks to us directly by voice into our spirit.

"Word of life"[5] is a term used in the Bible, referring not only to the Scriptures but also to the Living Word Himself, Jesus

Christ. A true follower of Christ not only loves and obeys the Scriptures, but also learns to *hear* His voice, and then through loving obedience do what He says.

God didn't intend that we only know His book. We're to personally get to know the Author Himself. By developing intimate dialogue with Him, our experiential spiritual growth accelerates. We must turn over the reigns of our lives from our own hands to His, and learn to do what He says—both from the Scriptures and via His voice in the spirit.

If we want more peace in our lives, what better teacher could we have than the Prince of Peace Himself?

In Part Two we'll explore some of the many ways we develop a lifestyle of peace in Jesus Christ.

~ Part Two ~

10 Ways Jesus Can Give You Peace

Our peace can never be more secure—
than that on which it depends.
~J.R. Miller[1]

CHAPTER 5

Yoked With the Master

Then Jesus said, "Come to me, all of you who are weary and carry heavy burdens, and I will give you rest. Take my yoke upon you. Let me teach you, because I am humble and gentle at heart, and you will find rest for your souls. For my yoke is easy to bear, and the burden I give you is light." (Matthew 11:28-30)

When the burdens of life tire us out and leave us drained, we often quote this familiar passage of Scripture. Many Christians turn to God for help only when life becomes overwhelming and too much to handle on their own. But perhaps Jesus is inviting us to partner with Him in the easier times as well.

Let's look closer at what our Lord is telling us in this passage.

Come to me, all of you who are weary and carry heavy burdens

Jesus is inviting those who are tired and weary to come to Him. As He lays out the parameters for His power in the verses preceding this section, we see that although all are called to "come," not all do.

At that time Jesus prayed this prayer: "O Father, Lord of heaven and earth, thank you for hiding these things from those who think themselves wise and clever, and for revealing them to the childlike. Yes, Father, it pleased you to do it this way! My Father has entrusted everything to me. No one truly knows the Son except the Father, and no one truly knows the Father except the Son and those to whom the Son chooses to reveal him." (Matthew 11:25-27)

Jesus is calling people who have been working hard and are exhausted. Perhaps they've had misguided priorities, or have been doing the wrong things. For too long they've been acting single-handedly, by their strength alone. Whatever the reason, their efforts have left them burdened down and depleted.

. . . and I will give you rest.

Jesus is summoning these wearied souls to come to Him for rest, relief, and refreshment. The whole passage is about work. In the next verse He refers to a yoke, which is a farming, or work tool. Jesus doesn't promise us an end from work, but a refreshing that empowers us to do His work.

Notice the many times the pronouns "me," "I," and "my" are used throughout the passage, making clear that Jesus Christ is the only way to find this rest.

Take my yoke upon you.

A yoke is a wooden harness that joins two animals such as oxen together so they can share the workload and become more productive. Neither animal could carry the load alone, but joined together they can shoulder the load with ease.

34

In biblical times yoke for oxen were often custom made to fit particular animals. It is believed that Jesus came from a carpenter's family, so it's likely he had personal experience in hand carving wooden yokes and making sure they fit well.

Using the illustration of a yoke, Jesus is inviting us to be partners with Him in the work of carrying out the Father's business in our lives.

Let me teach you, because I am humble and gentle at heart, and you will find rest for your souls.

Jesus asks us to come and learn from Him. In John 14, while still on the earth, Jesus spoke of a day coming when He would be gone physically, yet would be with us by way of the gift of the Holy Spirit.

*If you love me, obey my commandments. And I will ask the Father, and he will give you another **Advocate**, who will never leave you. He is the Holy Spirit, who leads into all truth. The world cannot receive him, because it isn't looking for him and doesn't recognize him. But you know him, because he lives with you now and later will be in you.*

No, I will not abandon you as orphans—I will come to you. Soon the world will no longer see me, but you will see me. Since I live, you also will live. When I am raised to life again, you will know that I am in my Father, and you are in me. Since I live, you also will live. When I am raised to life again, you will know that I am in my Father, and you are in me, and I am in you. Those who accept my commandments and obey them are the ones who love me. *And because they love me, my Father will love them. And I will love them and reveal myself to each of them. (John 14:15-21)*

The word "Advocate" is the Greek word *paraclete*. In other translations the word "Comforter" or "Counselor" is used. *Paraclete* comes from the word *parakletos*, meaning one who consoles, comforts, encourages, or uplifts. It can also mean one called to another person's side or aid, or one who intercedes on a person's behalf as an advocate in court.[1]

The word *paraclete* is in the passive form, which signifies "one called to the side of another"—like the two joined by a yoke. Jesus' relationship with us is meant to be one of sharing. Life is no longer just about me, but I am now in partnership with Him.

> *Jesus replied, "All who love me will do what I say. My Father will love them, and we will come and make our home with each of them. Anyone who doesn't love me will not obey me. And remember, my words are not my own. What I am telling you is from the Father who sent me. I am telling you these things now while I am still with you.* **But when the Father sends the Advocate [paraclete] as my representative—that is, the Holy Spirit—he will teach you everything and will remind you of everything I have told you."** *(John 14:23-26)*

Jesus Christ, by way of the Advocate—the Holy Spirit—is with us today, equipping us, teaching us, and guiding us.

"Let me teach you"—Jesus Christ clearly wants us to learn from Him. We are to work together with Him in an ongoing

relationship and learn to do things His way. As we lean on Him and allow Him to share our burdens and our work, we become more like Him, *"humble and gentle at heart."* We also find rest and refreshment for our souls.

For my yoke is easy to bear . . .

The yoke that Jesus gives us is easy, not burdensome. It fits well. It's been specially made for you alone to be shared with Him. Each Christian has a custom fitted ministry and purpose in life to carry out with the Lord. Doing the work without Him becomes burdensome, but shared with Him is done with ease.

. . . and the burden I give you is light.

Some theologians think the "burden" or "heavy load" in this section of Scripture may be referring to the many stipulations the Pharisees had added to the Old Testament Law. These conditions were intended to make the Law more applicable to everyday life, but in reality made it difficult and impractical. This form of legalistic Judaism missed God's intent for the Law, which was justice, mercy, and faith. In contrast, Jesus is saying His "burden" is light.

> *Doing the work without Him becomes burdensome, but shared with Him is done with ease.*

From his abundance we have all received one gracious blessing after another.[2] For the law was given through Moses, but God's unfailing love and faithfulness came through Jesus Christ. (John 1:16-17)

With the coming of Christ, God now invites us to experience grace. He doesn't want us to be loaded down with unnecessary religious protocols that may cause us to miss living in His grace, and enjoying His peace.

Clearly this magnificent section of Scripture implies a continuing relationship with Jesus Christ. We each have a yoke and a burden—a function and a responsibility as followers of Christ. When we find ourselves weary and weighted down with life and ministry, the remedy is found in bringing our hearts back into His presence. Carrying out our work with Jesus alongside us sharing the load is not tiresome or burdensome.

We find rest for our souls.

~ CHAPTER 6 ~

A Prayer-Full Life

In August 1877 Christian evangelist George Muller and his wife set sail from England to the United States aboard the SS Sardinian. While crossing the Atlantic the weather turned cold and the ship ran into dense fog. Muller explained to the captain that he needed to be in Quebec the following afternoon for an appointment.

"It is impossible," said the captain. He explained that he was slowing the ship down for safety and that Muller's appointment would have to be missed.

"Very well," said Muller, "if your ship cannot take me, God will find some other way—I have never broken an engagement for fifty-two years. Let us go down into the chart-room and pray."

The captain followed him down, claiming it would be a waste of time. Muller replied, " . . . my eye is not on the density of the fog, but on the living God, who controls every circumstance of my life."

After Muller prayed, the captain was about to but Muller stopped him. "First, you do not believe He will; and second, I believe He has, and there is no need whatever for you to pray about it."

"Captain," he continued, "I have known my Lord for fifty-two years, and there has never been a single day that I have failed to get an audience with the King. Get up, captain, and open the door, and you will find the fog is gone."

The captain opened the door. The fog had lifted. Shortly afterward the captain became a Christian and was later described by a well-known evangelist as "one of the most devoted men I ever knew."[1]

During his lifetime, George Muller[2] cared for more than 10,000 orphans as the director of the Ashley Down orphanage in Bristol, England. He also provided Christian education to over 120,000 children in the 117 schools he established.

But Muller is best known as a man of great faith and prayer, who talked to God about everything, and expected God to answer every prayer. His simple trust in God for every daily provision is truly inspiring.

How does one gain such a confident faith in the Almighty? The answer is simple: make prayer a way of life. Jesus is our greatest example of this kind of close communion with the Father.

Prayer Defines Our Relationship With God

A prayerful life begins with a decision that prayer is a priority. How important is your relationship with the Heavenly Father and with His Son Jesus Christ? Just as the lover yearns to be with the beloved, and always has him or her in mind, so we should yearn for God's fellowship because of our love for Him and His great love for us.

Francis de Sales[3] said, *"Every Christian needs a half-hour of prayer each day, except when he is busy, then he needs an hour."*

Like any other endeavor in life, if it becomes important enough to us we make time for it. Jesus prioritized His love for the Father by spending much time in prayer. As a result, He knew what the Father was doing in the world around Him, as well as what the Father was calling Him to do.

Jesus often got up early, went to a quiet place and spent time in prayer. Other times He spent the whole night in prayer.

Before daybreak the next morning, Jesus got up and went out to an isolated place to pray. (Mark 1:35)

One day soon afterward Jesus went up on a mountain to pray, and he prayed to God all night. (Luke 6:12)

If time with the Father was this important to Jesus, certainly we can learn from His example. Jesus didn't wait for a crisis to hit before He turned to God. Instead, He had a walking, talking love relationship with the Father daily. Jesus knew that God was with Him every moment, and that without Him He could do nothing.

So Jesus explained, "I tell you the truth, the Son can do nothing by himself. He does only what he sees the Father doing. Whatever the Father does, the Son also does." (John 5:19)

Jesus asks us to do likewise. He says that whatever we see Him (Jesus) do, we can do the same—and even greater!

I tell you the truth, anyone who believes in me will do the same works I have done, and even greater works, because I am going to be with the Father. You can ask for anything in my name, and I will do it, so that the Son can bring glory to the Father. Yes, ask me for anything in my name, and I will do it! (John 14:12-14)

Simply put, prayer is talking with God. It defines our relationship with Him. Prayer isn't to inform God of things that He may not be aware of, or to try and convince Him of things He already knows. Through prayer we express our devotion and love to the Father. We pour out our thoughts, desires, feelings, concerns, burdens, and disappointments—as well as our gratitude and praise.

Prayer is fellowship with God through Jesus Christ. A life of prayer is a Christ-centered life. We carve out time daily to read God's Word and learn His heart. As we approach its pages with a humble and inquiring heart through prayer, Jesus, by way of the Holy Spirit, gives us understanding.[4]

Prayer unleashes God's power and enables Him to go to work in our lives. Through prayer, we recognize His place in our lives. A believer draws near to the Father and gains direction for his or her life through prayer. It could be said that God has limited His power in our lives in proportion to the importance we place on prayer.

Prayer opens the doors to His blessings. It invites God to do what He's been longing to do all the time. Prayer aligns our will with His. Even when we don't see anything significant happening, by faith we trust He is at work.

Prayer has many aspects, including praise, confession, thanksgiving, petition, and intercession. Jesus asks us to pray to the Father "in His name." Since sin is what separates us from the Father, praying in the name of Jesus Christ acknowledges that Christ is the mediator who restores our fellowship with God.

> *Prayer in His name is more than simply saying the words "in the name of Jesus Christ" at the end of our prayers.*

Prayer in His name is more than simply tacking the words "in the name of Jesus Christ" at the end of our prayers. It's praying with the heart realization that our sufficiency is found in Christ alone. This recognition should characterize our prayers. It allows us the highest privilege in coming to God. It provides the key to every spiritual treasure.

Enter His Presence With Praise

The more intimately we know God, the greater should be our desire to worship Him, for He alone deserves all of our devotion and praise. In worshipping Him we acknowledge that He is great, and we are not. He is big, and we are small. He is powerful, and we are powerless.

43

This is what the LORD says: "Don't let the wise boast in their wisdom, or the powerful boast in their power, or the rich boast in their riches. But those who wish to boast should boast in this alone: that they truly know me and understand that I am the LORD who demonstrates unfailing love and who brings justice and righteousness to the earth, and that I delight in these things." (Jeremiah 9:23-24)

Psalms tells us that we enter His presence through thanksgiving and praise. We are to give thanks to Him continually for His goodness.

Enter his gates with thanksgiving; go into his courts with praise. Give thanks to him and praise his name. (Psalm 100:4)

. . . And You Will Have Peace
Dale Carnegie was once asked, *"What is the secret to your life?"* He replied, *"Every day I pray. I yield myself to God, the tensions and anxieties go out of me and peace and power come in."* [5]

Submit to God, and you will have peace; then things will go well for you. (Job 22:21)

Prayer At Its Highest
Any good ongoing relationship requires time and commitment. When interviewed, couples married 40, 50, or even 60 years all said that despite their shared history, they were

44

still changing and learning new things about themselves and each other.[6] Most happily married couples will tell you that they have learned to listen to their spouse (I didn't say "agree" but "listen.") Relationship is not a one-way monologue, but an ongoing shared dialogue.

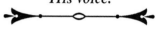

As we share ourselves in relationship with Christ, the ears of our hearts remain open to His voice.

What about our relationship with the Creator of the universe? Learning to know Him and hear His voice is a lifetime endeavor, and a journey that marks the Christian life with its greatest joy.

Learning to listen is an aspect of prayer that is often overlooked. Evangelical Christian missionary Frank C. Laubach[7] said, *"Prayer at its highest is a two-way conversation and for me the most important part is listening to God's replies."*

As we share ourselves in relationship with God through Christ, the ears of our hearts remain open to His voice. Quietly sitting in the Lord's presence and listening to Him speak should be part of our daily prayer time.

Final Thoughts

George Muller devoted much time to prayer. Again and again, he saw needs met—from provisions for meals at the orphanage to the fog being lifted so he could make an appointment. Muller's child-like trust and heartfelt devotion to the Heavenly Father through prayer serves as an inspiration to us all.

Those persons who know the deep peace of God, the unfathomable peace that passeth all understanding, are always men and women of much prayer. ~R.A. Torrey[8]

CHAPTER 7

Heading East, Heading West

In *A Forgiving God in an Unforgiving World*, Ron Lee Davis recounts the true story of a priest in the Philippines who carried in his heart the burden of a secret sin he had committed many years before. Although he had repented, he still had no peace in his heart, no sense of God's forgiveness.

In his church there was a woman who claimed to have visions in which she spoke to Christ and He with her. Being skeptical, the priest decided to test her. So he said, "The next time you speak with Christ, I want you to ask Him what sin your priest committed while he was in seminary." The woman agreed.

A few days later the priest asked, "Well, did Christ visit you in your dreams?" "Yes, he did," she replied. "And did you ask Him what sin I committed in seminary?" "Yes." "Well, what did He say?" "He said, 'I don't remember'."[1]

———————⟨≈⟩———————

God's unfathomable forgiveness is as the woman stated—what He forgives, He forgets. This is a difficult concept for our human understanding. The devil remembers our sins and tries to bring shame or guilt with their memories. Yet the truth that God remembers our sins no more is something we need to believe and trust.

And I will forgive their wickedness, and I will never again remember their sins. (Hebrews 8:12)[2]

As Far As the East is From the West
The LORD is compassionate and merciful, slow to get angry and filled with unfailing love. He will not constantly accuse us, nor remain angry forever. He does not punish us for all our sins; he does not deal harshly with us, as we deserve. For his unfailing love toward those who fear him is as great as the height of the heavens above the earth. **He has removed our sins as far from us as the east is from the west.** *(Psalm 103:8-12)*

Start at any location on a world globe and travel east. You will continue east indefinitely. Same if you travel west. But not so if you travel north or south. If you continue north long enough eventually you'll start heading south. But the east and the west never meet. That's how far God has removed our sins from us! Clearly, they are so far removed they will no longer come to remembrance.

If the garbage in a trashcan represents our sins, the lid can be put on it to cover what's within. The sins are still in there, but they're hidden with the lid on. In Christ, the rubbish is not simply hidden, but removed, and the inside of the can thoroughly cleaned out before putting the lid on. This is the remission of sins for which Christ shed His blood on the cross.

For this is My blood of the new covenant, which is shed
for many for the remission of sins. (Matt. 26:28 NKJV)

In Christ, our sins are wiped clean and no longer
remembered. An important part of faith is accepting our
forgiveness in Christ.

Accepting Christ's Forgiveness

Living life with forgiveness allows us to have peace by
freeing us up on the inside. It releases the bitterness we often
hold on to in our hearts because of people or situations that have
hurt us. Although at times it is difficult to put forgiveness into
practice, it begins with the recognition and acceptance of
Christ's forgiveness of us.

You were dead because of your sins and because your
sinful nature was not yet cut away. Then God made you
alive with Christ, for he forgave all our sins. (Col. 2:13)

He is so rich in kindness and grace that he purchased our
freedom with the blood of his Son and forgave our sins.
(Ephesians 1:7)

I—yes, I alone—will blot out your sins for my own
sake and will never think of them again. (Isaiah 43:25)

Christ, through His love and obedience to the Father,
forgave all of our sins of the past, and still forgives us today. God
understands that as new creations in Christ we are still imperfect
people and will sin in our walks with Him.

Children sometimes misbehave. When they do, they are still sons or daughters of their parents. That never changes. But at that moment, their relationship with mom and dad is damaged. At times there are consequences for their actions. Yet reconciliation between parents and children through forgiveness of the wrongdoing must occur to fully restore the relationship.

1 John 1:9 tells us that God is faithful to forgive.

But if we confess our sins to him, he is faithful and just to forgive us our sins and to cleanse us from all wickedness.

Through confession and forgiveness, God restores our broken fellowship (relationship) with Him, and welcomes us back into His presence. Knowing we are forgiven for all (yes, *all*) our sins should bring great peace to our hearts.

Forgiving Ourselves

Is there something in your past that you know God has forgiven you for, yet it still troubles you? When you think of it, you feel uneasy and not at peace? It could be you have not yet forgiven yourself.

"But Lord, I don't *feel* I can forgive myself!" Why? Because you have believed your feelings more than Scripture.

Jesus wants you to give Him *all* your pain. He'll take your shame, your bitterness from you. Go to the Lord and repent for holding on to the pain, the bitterness, or whatever you are feeling, and not trusting Him enough.

Give your burdens to the LORD, and he will take care of you. (Psalm 55:22a)

Ask Him to help you see yourself as He does and help you forgive yourself. Accept His love, grace, and forgiveness in the situation. We must not allow the devil to keep reminding us of our past indiscretions to the extent that it deters us from living for the Lord.

In a dream, Martin Luther found himself being attacked by satan. The devil unrolled a long scroll containing a list of Luther's sins and held it before him. On reaching the end of the scroll Luther asked the devil, "Is that all?" "No," came the reply, and a second scroll was thrust in front of him. Then, after a second came a third. But now the devil had no more. "You've forgotten something," Luther exclaimed triumphantly. "Quickly write on each of them, 'The blood of Jesus Christ, God's Son, cleanses us from all sins.'"[3]

Only once you release the weight of the sin you've been holding onto, and forgive yourself, are you truly accepting Christ's sacrifice for your sins.

Only once you release the weight of the sin you've been holding onto, and forgive yourself, are you truly accepting Christ's sacrifice for your sins.

Change My Heart, O God

We read in Psalm 51 David's emotional response and heartfelt cries to God. May our hearts echo his pleas each day—regardless of our transgressions!

Have mercy on me, O God, because of your unfailing love. Because of your great compassion, blot out the stain of my sins. Wash me clean from my guilt. Purify me from my sin. For I recognize my rebellion; it haunts me day and night. Against you, and you alone, have I sinned; I have done what is evil in your sight. You will be proved right in what you say, and your judgment against me is just. For I was born a sinner—yes, from the moment my mother conceived me. But you desire honesty from the womb, teaching me wisdom even there.

Purify me from my sins, and I will be clean; wash me, and I will be whiter than snow. Oh, give me back my joy again; you have broken me— now let me rejoice. Don't keep looking at my sins. Remove the stain of my guilt. Create in me a clean heart, O God. Renew a loyal spirit within me. Do not banish me from your presence, and don't take your Holy Spirit from me.

Restore to me the joy of your salvation, and make me willing to obey you. Then I will teach your ways to rebels, and they will return to you. Forgive me for shedding blood, O God who saves; then I will joyfully sing of your forgiveness. (Psalm 51:1-14)

Of ourselves we are nothing. Only in Him do we experience wholeness. May our prayers resonate with King David's—*"create in me a clean heart, O God"* . . . *"wash me clean from my guilt; purify me from my sin."*

By accepting God's forgiveness—and forgiving ourselves—we can again experience His peace and His joy in our hearts.

> *"Restore to me the joy of your salvation . . . I will joyfully sing of your forgiveness."*

CHAPTER 8

Letting Go of the Rope

Extending the spiritual grace of forgiveness is an art every Christian needs to develop if we are to live as Christ in this world. As important as accepting our forgiveness in Christ and forgiving ourselves is, we must learn to forgive others as well. In fact, Jesus says if we don't forgive others, our Heavenly Father will not forgive us.

If you forgive those who sin against you, your heavenly Father will forgive you. But if you refuse to forgive others, your Father will not forgive your sins. (Matthew 6:14-15)

Make allowance for each other's faults, and forgive anyone who offends you. Remember, the Lord forgave you, so you must forgive others. (Colossians 3:13)

Forgiving Others, That We May be Forgiven

How can our hearts be in harmony with the Lord if we're harboring grievances about others? Didn't Christ die for them, too? Forgiveness is often difficult—sometimes extremely difficult—but is not optional behavior for the Christian. If we truly desire to live a holy life we must obey the Lord's command to forgive others. No matter how tough or unjust the situation may be—even if we might still be living out the consequences of it—the Lord says we must forgive.

In his book *The Letter to the Hebrews*, William Barclay says forgiveness is the most costly thing in the world. He writes:

> *Human forgiveness is costly. A son or a daughter may go wrong; a father or a mother may forgive; but that forgiveness has brought tears . . . There was a price of a broken heart to pay. Divine forgiveness is costly. God is love, but God is holiness. God, least of all, can break the great moral laws on which the universe is built.*

> *Sin must have its punishment or the very structure of life disintegrates. And God alone can pay the terrible price that is necessary before men can be forgiven. Forgiveness is never a case of saying: "It's all right; it doesn't matter." It is the most costly thing in the world. Without the shedding of the heart's blood, there can be no forgiveness of sins.*

> *Nothing brings people to their senses with such arresting violence as seeing the effect of their sin on someone who loves them in this world or on the God who loves them forever, and to say to themselves: "It cost that to forgive my sins."*[1]

Forgiving doesn't excuse or justify what someone has done to you—but it does protect your heart. Often the offending person is not even aware of the pain you are going through caused by your lack of forgiveness. The one hurt the most by harboring bitterness and unforgiveness is yourself. Lack of forgiveness gives advantage to the devil and his evil schemes.[2] The resulting bitterness defiles or pollutes our souls.

> *Look after each other so that none of you fails to receive the grace of God. Watch out that no poisonous root of bitterness grows up to trouble you, corrupting many. (Hebrews 12:15)*

When you have truly forgiven someone you no longer respond with resentment or bitterness. You can think of the person with no ill feelings. Forgiveness releases the bitterness and replaces it with peace.

Isn't that what our new life in Christ is all about? In and of ourselves we struggle to forgive. But with His help we can forgive. Forgiveness is an act of faith. It is

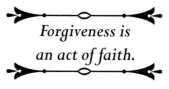

Forgiveness is an act of faith.

recognizing that God works out the ultimate justice, and it is not up to me to decide. By forgiving another, I relinquish my right to retaliation and trust that God will take care of all matters of fairness.

As humans we may never be able to forget as God does when He forgives, but in time we will see the hurts in our lives healed over and just the scars remain. An open wound hurts to the touch, but a scar does not. It is seen but not felt.

Corrie ten Boom[3] was a dedicated Dutch Christian who was imprisoned for helping many Jews escape the Nazi Holocaust during World War II. Her famous book *The Hiding Place* tells of the ordeal.

Corrie tells of not being able to forget a wrong that had been done to her. She had forgiven the person, but she kept rehashing the incident and couldn't sleep. In desperation, she cried out to God for help in putting the problem to rest.

"His help came in the form of a kindly Lutheran pastor," Corrie wrote, "to whom I confessed my failure after two sleepless weeks."

"Up in the church tower," he said, nodding out the window, "is a bell which is rung by pulling on a rope. But you know what? After the sexton lets go of the rope, the bell keeps on swinging. First ding, then dong. Slower and slower until there's a final dong and it stops.

I believe the same thing is true of forgiveness. When we forgive, we take our hand off the rope. But if we've been tugging at our grievances for a long time, we mustn't be surprised if the old angry thoughts keep coming for a while. They're just the ding-dongs of the old bell slowing down."

Corrie shares, "And so it proved to be. There were a few more midnight reverberations, a couple of dings when the subject came up in my conversations, but the force— which was my willingness in the matter—had gone out of them. They came less and less often and at the last stopped altogether: we can trust God not only above our emotions, but also above our thoughts."[4]

Letting Go

With Jesus' help our hearts can be cleansed, and we can experience the healing power of forgiveness. Although the dings and dongs may still reverberate for a time afterward, we know that in time, they will stop. With His help alone we can move on into newfound peace in our lives.

Christian teacher and author Roy L. Smith offers the following (paraphrased) suggestions to help us forgive others:

- Begin by assuring yourself that compared to Christ's suffering you haven't been seriously wronged at all.
- Recall the many kind deeds that have been shown to you, perhaps even by the person who has harmed you.
- List the benefits you have received from the Lord.
- Thank Him for blessing you with His love and forgiveness each day.
- Make an honest effort to pray for the one who injured you.
- Go even further by looking for an opportunity to help the person.
- If the offense is especially hard to forget, try to erase the memory by thinking gracious thoughts, especially meaningful Bible verses.
- Finally, before you fall asleep at night, repeat slowly and thoughtfully the phrase from the Lord's Prayer, ". . . *forgive us our sins, as we have forgiven those who sin against us."*

Unforgiveness pulls us away from Christ and robs us of the sweetness of His fellowship. It prevents us from finding peace. If you are wrestling with forgiving someone, repent and pour out your heart to the Lord today. If possible, go to the person and seek reconciliation by sharing with them how they have hurt you. Offer your forgiveness. If this is not possible, relinquish it to the Lord and seek His strength to forgive.

He understands, and will help you let go of the rope.

CHAPTER 9

A Royal Wardrobe

As we busily move through our days, it is easy to become immersed in our own worlds. There are meetings at work, bills to pay, kids to pick up, meals to make. So many responsibilities, so little time. For many of us, carving out that quiet time with the Lord is a challenge, and must be done first thing in the morning, or it just doesn't happen. So we do the best we can, enjoy His presence through our days, and remain active in His service. Bumps in the road come along, but with the Lord's help we make it through. Life is good. We are thankful.

Suddenly one day something major happens in the world, and we're jolted into remembering the "big picture."

A school shooting. Hurricane devastation. 9/11.

We realize what little control we really have, even as Christians. We ponder the evil in the world, and our thoughts turn to the end-time events and the promised return of Christ. How we yearn for that day! And we take comfort in the fact that the sovereign God of the universe is in charge, not us.

But what about when the attacks and conflicts become personal? The guy at work who always gives you a hard time . . .

the person at the gym who makes cruel comments about your weight . . . the friend who speaks lies about your achievements.

Ephesians 6:12 gives us the crucial reminder that the fight we're in is not person against person, but spiritual. Life is a spiritual reality, and we are in a spiritual war against real enemies of the spirit realm.

> *For we are not fighting against flesh-and-blood enemies, but against evil rulers and authorities of the unseen world, against mighty powers in this dark world, and against evil spirits in the heavenly places.*

The context of this verse paints an even bigger picture of how we should live as Christ followers in this world. We are to "put on" the armor of God to be victors in this life and to show His love to the world.

> *A final word: Be strong in the Lord and in his mighty power. **Put on all of God's armor so that you will be able to stand firm against all strategies of the devil.** For we are not fighting against flesh-and-blood enemies, but against evil rulers and authorities of the unseen world, against mighty powers in this dark world, and against evil spirits in the heavenly places.*

> *Therefore, put on every piece of God's armor so you will be able to resist the enemy in the time of evil. Then after the battle you will be standing firm. Stand your ground, putting on the **belt of truth** and the **body armor of God's righteousness.** **For shoes, put on the peace** that comes from the Good News so that you will be fully prepared. In*

*addition to all of these, hold up **the shield of faith** to stop the fiery arrows of the devil. Put on **salvation as your helmet**, and take **the sword of the Spirit**, which is the word of God. Pray in the Spirit at all times and on every occasion. Stay alert and be persistent in your prayers for all believers everywhere. (Ephesians 6:10-17)*

Most of us approach life as beings of body and soul who also happen to have a Spirit. Perhaps it would do us good to view ourselves the other way—*as spiritual beings who happen to have a body and soul.*

A Spiritual Perspective on Life Gives Us Peace

Satan's schemes are constantly seeking to steal, kill, and destroy God's people.[1] But with a godly, spiritual perspective on life, daily challenges become opportunities to draw closer to Him. Worldly events don't shake us, because we know who is ultimately in charge. Attacks, though painful for the moment, grow small in light of eternity. The Bible assures us that as we seek His face, we are promised victory in all of life's situations.

Most of us approach life as beings of body and soul who also happen to have a Spirit.

We are told to "put on" the following armor of God:

- Belt of TRUTH
- Breastplate of RIGHTEOUSNESS
- Sandals of PEACE

- Shield of FAITH
- Helmet of SALVATION
- Sword of the Spirit—GOD'S WORD

Applying God's armor ensures success in the spiritual battle of this life. We find peace knowing that the Lord Jesus Christ is working with us, and in Him we are victorious. The armor is more than just a protective covering—it's the very life of Christ Himself. He becomes our refuge, our hiding place, our shelter in the storm. Jesus not only covers us as a shield, He fills us with His life.

As we live in the protective covering of the armor—in the presence of Christ—we also experience oneness with Him. Life is no longer about simply fulfilling our own desires, but about allowing ourselves to be transformed into His likeness so we may carry out His work in the world.

Clothe Yourself With the Presence of Christ

Romans 13:12-14 says we are to "clothe" ourselves with Christ's presence:

The night is almost gone; the day of salvation will soon be here. So remove your dark deeds like dirty clothes, and **put on the shining armor of right living.** *Because we belong to the day, we must live decent lives for all to see. Don't participate in the darkness of wild parties and drunkenness, or in sexual promiscuity and immoral living, or in quarreling and jealousy. Instead,* **clothe yourself with the presence of the Lord Jesus Christ.** *And don't let yourself think about ways to indulge your evil desires.*

A Royal Wardrobe

"Clothe yourself with the presence of the Lord Jesus Christ." What a wonderful mind picture! Surely we wouldn't consider going out into the world without clothes on. Yet how often do we venture out without our spiritual clothes on—the presence of Christ?

Clothed with His presence, He partners with us through the trials and the triumphs of life. We share in His sufferings as well as His glory. He shares in ours.

> *Dear friends, don't be surprised at the fiery trials you are going through, as if something strange were happening to you. Instead, be very glad—for these trials make you **partners with Christ in his suffering, so that you will have the wonderful joy of seeing his glory** when it is revealed to all the world. (1 Peter 4:12-13)*

> *Since you have been raised to new life with Christ, set your sights on the realities of heaven, where Christ sits in the place of honor at God's right hand. Think about the things of heaven, not the things of earth. For you died to this life, and your real life is hidden with Christ in God. And **when Christ, who is your life, is revealed to the whole world, you will share in all his glory.** (Colossians 3:1-4)*

What could be more glorious than sharing oneness with Jesus Christ! He is closer than your breath. Just a thought away. Always beckoning you, yearning for the pleasure of your company.

We are never alone. Just as putting on new clothes each morning is habit, so putting on Jesus Christ and connecting with

Him throughout each day becomes the very bedrock of our lives. We are united—combined into one—with Him.

*And all who have been united with Christ in baptism have **put on Christ, like putting on new clothes**. (Galatians 3:27)*

We sometimes hear stories of committed Christians who face torture for their faith. They often testify to supernatural strength—even joy—that enables them to endure inconceivable pain. How can this be? Only a close partnership with the Lord, and a trust in His presence and provision could give someone such amazing power.

Can anything ever separate us from Christ's love? Does it mean he no longer loves us if we have trouble or calamity, or are persecuted, or hungry, or destitute, or in danger, or threatened with death? (As the Scriptures say, "For your sake we are killed every day; we are being slaughtered like sheep.") No, despite all these things, overwhelming victory is ours through Christ, who loved us.

*And I am convinced that nothing can ever separate us from God's love. Neither death nor life, neither angels nor demons, neither our fears for today nor our worries about tomorrow—not even the powers of hell can separate us from God's love. No power in the sky above or in the earth below—indeed, **nothing in all creation will ever be able to separate us from the love of God that is revealed in Christ Jesus our Lord**. (Romans 8:35-39)*

Christ doesn't promise us the absence of pain, but rather offers us victory in all life's struggles. Nothing, absolutely nothing can separate us from His love. Clothing ourselves with His presence enables us to share His love with others, which binds us together.

Since God chose you to be the holy people he loves, you must **clothe yourselves with tenderhearted mercy, kindness, humility, gentleness, and patience.**
Above all, **clothe yourselves with love,** *which binds us all together in perfect harmony. (Colossians 3:12,14)*

Putting on the Armor Daily

Each day we are to put on Christ Jesus the Lord, not by simply reciting the parts of the armor, but by entering into a continuing relationship with the Heavenly Father through Him.

We put **truth** on in our hearts and minds and stand firmly upon it. We rely on the **righteousness** we have in Him. We see ourselves as He does and walk as He walked, displaying "right living." We share the message of the gospel of **peace** with people we come in contact

As Christians living with the armor of God, we should so present Christ to the world that our own selves are hidden from view.

with. We endeavor to walk by **faith** and not by sight, trusting in Him. We're mindful of our **salvation**—past, present, and future. We quietly listen to His **words** to us, so we might live a life of glorious victory through Him.

When medieval knights prepared for battle and donned full suits of armor, it was nearly impossible to see who they really were. Their knightship became their new persona. As Christians living with the armor of God, we should so present Christ to the world that our own selves are hidden from view.

As Christ is all of the armor, He is each individual part. Let's prayerfully look at each piece of the armor we are to put on to be victors in the spiritual battle of life. As you continue through this section, I invite you to personalize the following prayers and declarations of faith.

Belt of Truth: God's truth, as revealed in the Scriptures and

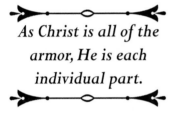

As Christ is all of the armor, He is each individual part.

through His Son, becomes the reference point and filter for all I see, hear, believe, and do. Literally, Jesus Christ is the all truth.[2] Putting on the belt of truth, I make His thoughts my own.

Thank you Father for revealing the truth about yourself, and your will for me in your Holy Scriptures. Thank you for your Son Jesus Christ, who tasted my humanity, yet never sinned. By your grace and goodness you lead me through all of life's circumstances. May your truth be the belt that holds all my other clothes in place. As I put it on in my mind and heart this day, may it be the gauge against which I measure all of life. In the name of Jesus Christ, Amen.

Breastplate of Righteousness: The righteousness I have in Christ causes me to stand unblemished, blameless, and beautiful before my Lord. Wearing this breastplate, the attacks of others hold no ground. Mindful of my righteousness, there is no room for condemnation. Christ is my righteousness!

Father, thank you for helping me realize that without you I am nothing. On my own there are not enough good works I could do to be worthy to stand in your presence. Lord, thank you for taking my sins to the cross and offering me your perfect, righteous life in return. Show me if I have fallen short in any way, and if there is anything I need to confess to you right now—so that nothing should hinder me from the joy of your presence. Thank you for forgiving me and filling me with the righteousness I have through you. Refresh me and renew me so that I may show your righteous life to the world. In the name of Jesus Christ, Amen.

Sandals of Peace: As the Prince of Peace quietly speaks reminders of His presence, my heart fills with His peace. With Christ going with me today, I can carry His peace to the world as I put on His shoes.

Father, thank you for the peace you give me when I put my trust in you and you alone. As I walk out into the world, I know you go with me. There is nothing to fear. Keep me still in your presence as we work together today. Let your peace flow through me that I may carry it to others and lead them to you. In the name of Jesus Christ, Amen.

Shield of Faith: As the Author and finisher of my faith, Christ is also my shield of faith. The faith of my Lord Jesus Christ is in me, shielding me from doubt and despair. Through Him I can do all things. This faith is my undisturbed believing in the presence of the King.

Thank you Father for helping me put my faith and trust in you and you alone. No matter what comes my way, I declare your sovereignty, truth, and precious promises. Help me be still to hear what you have for me today, that I might walk, displaying your power to those around me. In the name of Jesus Christ, Amen.

Helmet of Salvation: Jesus Christ is my past, present, and future salvation. Through Him, I'm already saved from guilt and condemnation; He saves me today from every trial; and one day in the future I will exchange this decaying, defective body for a new, perfect body like His. Wearing these thoughts serves as protection from all that goes on inside my head.

Heavenly Father, I rejoice that the promise of salvation is not only for yesterday's failures or today's battles, but for the joy we will share for all eternity. Show me how to wear my salvation so that others may see the light of your presence in me. As I put on the helmet of salvation, guard my thoughts with your protective covering. I count on you to bring me safely and successfully through every challenge of today. Anchor my heart in the comforting hope of my ultimate salvation, which will bring me face to face with my King. In the name of Jesus Christ, Amen.

Sword of the Spirit—the Word of God: As the only offensive piece of armor, the Sword of the Spirit is the word (*rhema*³) of God—the Lord's speaking to me. Jesus Christ, through His still, quiet voice, gives me all I need moment by moment to walk confidently and triumphantly through every battle of life. The words I hear Him speak are my offense.

Thank you Father for speaking to me through your Holy Spirit. May your words help me triumph in my thoughts and emotions and keep my trust in you. As we walk through this day together, tell me your truths, that I may victoriously show your presence to the world. In the name of Jesus Christ, Amen.

Living in His Presence

Each morning, we can awaken with praise on the lips of our hearts for another new day. As we seek the Lord's presence, we are reassured that He is with us. What joy! We are never alone. With His help we dress our hearts for the day, securing each piece of the armor in place.

As we begin the day clothed in the presence of the King, wearing His royal wardrobe, we know that He will protect us against discouragement and the many destructive thoughts and feelings the world may throw our way. As we allow the Lord to be our protective covering, nothing will disturb the peace we find in His presence.

Though we may face struggles, He is able to bring victory in the midst of trials. As we yield ourselves to Him, He hides us under the shadow of His wing. Together, we face the storms of life. We feel the winds beating, but know we are safe. Though the tempest swirls all around us, we abide securely with the Lord in the eye of the storm—and in this quiet oasis there is rest. We take comfort in His nearness, as we share in His sufferings as well as His glory.

Throughout the day we partner with the Lord in bringing the gospel of peace to others . . . Together we share the pain of a friend, and bring the comfort of truth to a broken heart. The Lord gives us words to speak to a neighbor in need.

With the armor securely in place we are able to view life from His perspective and defeat every devilish attack. He enables us to see the rainbow behind every storm and find hope.

"Draw near, and seek My presence," He beckons each one of us. "For in the storms and spiritual battles of life, only in My presence will you find peace."

CHAPTER 10

Growing Giant Pumpkins

The thing I love best about living in northern New York is the changing seasons. Each has its own special beauty, yet autumn is by far my favorite. There's nothing quite like seeing the mountains ablaze with gold, crimson, and copper as the leaves begin to fall. The days are warm and pleasant and the nights crisp and cool. Roadside stands are bursting with apples, mums, cider donuts, and . . . pumpkins!

If you've ever grown pumpkins you have probably heard of Dill's Atlantic Giant variety of premium pumpkin seeds. From these seeds grow the giant pumpkins that set world records. In 2012, a pumpkin grown in Rhode Island was the first to weigh in at over two thousand pounds, setting a new world record. While much work is required to produce these giants, most growers will agree that soil condition is perhaps the most important ingredient. The soil must be cultivated correctly or the pumpkin just won't grow properly.[1] And while many people mistakenly believe pumpkins to be vegetables, they are in fact technically a fruit, because they contain seeds inside a fleshy edible body.

Fruit is mentioned in the Bible many times, both literally and figuratively. The concept of bearing fruit is used often. And just as with literal fruit, no fruit grows until seeds are planted.

The Sower and the Seed

In the gospels, Jesus tells the parable of the sower and the seed.[2] As a sower went out to sow seed, it fell on various types of ground. Some fell on a footpath where it was stepped on and birds devoured it before it could take root. Some ground was rocky and hard. Seeds sprouted, but the plants soon wilted and died because they lacked moisture. Other ground was receptive, but weeds and thorns grew and choked the tender plants. Some seed fell on fertile soil and produced abundant crops.

The seed represents the word (*logos*[3]) of God. In the second half of the parable, Jesus explains that this illustration demonstrates the different kinds of people who hear the gospel message, and the various results they reap.

This is the meaning of the parable: The seed is God's word. The seeds that fell on the footpath represent those who hear the message, only to have the devil come and take it away from their hearts and prevent them from believing and being saved. The seeds on the rocky soil represent those who hear the message and receive it with joy. But since they don't have deep roots, they believe for a while, then they fall away when they face temptation.

The seeds that fell among the thorns represent those who hear the message, but all too quickly the message is crowded out by the cares and riches and pleasures of this life. And so they never grow into maturity. And the seeds that fell on the good soil represent honest, good-hearted people who hear God's word, cling to it, and patiently produce a huge harvest. (Luke 8:11-15)

When the word of God (the seed) falls on "good ground," those who hear and keep the word in their hearts consequently harvest good fruit in their lives in abundance.[4]

Bearing Spiritual Fruit—Good or Bad

Scripture tells us that just as we identify a tree by its fruit, we identify people by the "fruit" that is seen in their lives—their actions. We will see either "bad fruit" or "good fruit," and it is determined to a large extent by the nourishment they receive, or what they feed on.[5]

You can identify them by their fruit, that is, by the way they act. Can you pick grapes from thornbushes, or figs from thistles? A good tree produces good fruit, and a bad tree produces bad fruit. A good tree can't produce bad fruit, and a bad tree can't produce good fruit. So every tree that does not produce good fruit is chopped down and thrown into the fire. Yes, just as you can identify a tree by its fruit, so you can identify people by their actions. (Matthew 7:16-20)

A good tree can't produce bad fruit, and a bad tree can't produce good fruit. A good person produces good things from the treasury of a good heart, and an evil person produces evil things from the treasury of an evil heart. What you say flows from what is in your heart. (Luke 6:43,45)

A godless, sinful, and selfish life produces bad or bitter fruit, as God declares in Proverbs 1:26-31:

> *So I will laugh when you are in trouble! I will mock you when disaster overtakes you—when calamity overtakes you like a storm, when disaster engulfs you like a cyclone, and anguish and distress overwhelm you. When they cry for help, I will not answer. Though they anxiously search for me, they will not find me. For they hated knowledge and chose not to fear the LORD. They rejected my advice and paid no attention when I corrected them. Therefore, **they must eat the bitter fruit of living their own way, choking on their own schemes.**

Conversely, those who delight in the ways of God and walk in righteousness and obedience to them prosper and bear good fruit. They are like well-nourished trees planted by a river, whose leaves do not wither.

> *But they delight in the law of the LORD, meditating on it day and night. They are like trees planted along the riverbank, **bearing fruit each season**. Their leaves never wither, and they prosper in all they do. (Psalm 1:2-3)*

What is in our hearts comes out of our mouths in words and is seen in our lives by actions. The true followers of Jesus Christ are those who bring forth good spiritual fruit—the kind that produces a huge harvest!

How to Bear Good Spiritual Fruit

John 15 gives a beautiful illustration of how we can bear fruit in our lives by *abiding in Jesus Christ*. As we go through some of this chapter together, I encourage you to take your time contemplating the deep and comforting words of Jesus.

> *I am the true grapevine, and my Father is the gardener. He cuts off every branch of mine that doesn't produce fruit, and he prunes the branches that do bear fruit so they will produce even more. You have already been pruned and purified by the message I have given you. Remain in me, and I will remain in you. For a branch cannot produce fruit if it is severed from the vine, and* **you cannot be fruitful unless you remain in me.** *Yes, I am the vine; you are the branches. Those who remain in me, and I in them, will produce much fruit. For apart from me you can do nothing. (John 15:1-5)*

A branch in and of itself does not bear fruit. It must be connected to the vine to receive nourishment. Through Jesus Christ (the vine) we receive the nourishment we need to bear fruit. Without Him, we bear no fruit and "can do nothing."

Our Heavenly Father is the gardener who tends to our spiritual fruit. A gardener removes the dead, fruitless plants from the garden. He also cuts back, or prunes the healthy branches so they remain strong and fruitful. Pruning a plant doesn't kill it. It simply wounds the plant for a short time so it might come back stronger.

If we stay connected to Jesus, we will bear good godly fruit. Dead leaves and weeds will be cleared out. As our branches are pruned we may find ourselves cut or wounded at times, but as we abide in Christ and take our nourishment from Him, we come back and grow healthier and stronger.

> *By abiding in Christ and subsequently bearing fruit, we carry out our primary purpose in life—glorifying God.*

Anyone who does not remain in me is thrown away like a useless branch and withers. Such branches are gathered into a pile to be burned. But if you remain in me and my words remain in you, you may ask for anything you want, and it will be granted! **When you produce much fruit, you are my true disciples. This brings great glory to my Father.** *(John 15:6-8)*

As we dwell in Christ we can ask anything according to God's will (His written Word) and it will be done for us. By abiding in Christ and subsequently bearing fruit, we carry out our primary purpose in life—glorifying God.

I have loved you even as the Father has loved me. Remain in my love. When you obey my commandments, you remain in my love, just as I obey my Father's commandments and remain in his love. I have told you these things so that you will be filled with my joy. Yes, your joy will overflow! This is my commandment: Love each other in the same way I have loved you. There is no greater love than to lay down one's life for one's friends. You are my friends if you do what I command. **I no longer call you slaves, because a master doesn't confide** *in his slaves. Now you are my friends, since I have told you everything the Father told me. (John 15:9-15)*

This section continues to exhort us toward an ongoing relationship with Christ—one that "abides in the vine" and subsequently bears fruit. Abiding in Christ we experience His joy, and our joy becomes full. We start to walk in His love, in His steps, not only in a servant/master relationship, but also as friends. A servant may not know what his master's intentions are, or why he is being asked to do something. Jesus calls us friends. Surely this implies communication with one another and a more intimate, sharing relationship. The best of friends will confide in one another the secrets of their hearts. Do you want to know that your life is pleasing to the Father? How wonderful that Jesus calls us friends as we carry out His commands and dwell in His presence!

*You didn't choose me. I chose you. **I appointed you to go and produce lasting fruit, so that the Father will give you whatever you ask for, using my name.***

But I will send you the Advocate—the Spirit of truth. He will come to you from the Father and will testify all about me. And you must also testify about me because you have been with me from the beginning of my ministry. (John 15:16, 26-27)

The gospels record Christ's earthly ministry. Here, at the end of John 15 Jesus is speaking of a time coming in the future—after His crucifixion and ascension—when the Holy Spirit (the Comforter or Advocate) would come and be present with all who believe in Him. This includes all those who have believed since Acts 2 (the day of Pentecost when the outpouring of the Holy Spirit was given) until His second coming, still in the future. This is the church to which you and I belong, the body of Christ, of which He is the head, and we are the members.

The Holy Spirit testifies to us of Jesus, and we are to testify Christ to the world by bearing good fruit. In this section, Jesus is again emphasizing the importance of a continuing relationship with Him.

An intimate walking-talking relationship with Jesus Christ affords us the means to bear good spiritual fruit in our lives—fruit that will bring glory to God.

Living by the Sinful Nature vs. Living by the Spirit

Let's look at the book of Galatians. At the time Paul wrote this epistle to the church at Galatia, many of the believers were still zealous for the Old Testament Law and had not yet experienced salvation by grace. This major theme—of living by the Law vs. living by the Spirit through faith—is seen throughout the epistle.

In chapter 5, Paul clearly exhorts the believers to "live by the Spirit" in this new life in Christ, to the end of bearing good spiritual fruit.

> *For if you are trying to make yourselves right with God by keeping the law, you have been cut off from Christ!*
> *For you have been called to live in freedom, my brothers and sisters. But don't use your freedom to satisfy your*

sinful nature. Instead, use your freedom to serve one another in love. (Galatians 5:4a, 13)

Next Paul contrasts in greater detail living by the Spirit and living by our old sinful nature—and defines the fruit of each.

Fruit of the Sinful Nature vs. Fruit of the Spirit

So I say, let the Holy Spirit guide your lives. Then you won't be doing what your sinful nature craves. The sinful nature wants to do evil, which is just the opposite of what the Spirit wants. And the Spirit gives us desires that are the opposite of what the sinful nature desires. These two forces are constantly fighting each other, so you are not free to carry out your good intentions.

But when you are directed by the Spirit, you are not under obligation to the law of Moses. When you follow the desires of your sinful nature, the results are very clear: sexual immorality, impurity, lustful pleasures, idolatry, sorcery, hostility, quarreling, jealousy, outbursts of anger, selfish ambition, dissension, division, envy, drunkenness, wild parties, and other sins like these. Let me tell you again, as I have before, that anyone living that sort of life will not inherit the Kingdom of God.

But the Holy Spirit produces this kind of fruit in our lives: love, joy, peace, patience, kindness, goodness, faithfulness, gentleness, and self-control. *There is no law against these things! Those who belong to Christ Jesus have nailed the passions and desires of their sinful nature* *to his cross and crucified them there. Since we are living by the Spirit, let us follow the Spirit's leading in every part of our lives. (Galatians 5:16-25)*

One Fruit, Nine Attributes

The Greek word for "fruit"[6] is in the singular, indicating there is one fruit with nine attributes, or characteristics: love, joy, *peace*, patience, kindness, goodness, faithfulness, gentleness, and self-control. These characteristics reflect the quality of our lives spiritually, or our relationship with Christ.

Galatians 5 shows us that to live by the Spirit is to live in love. Our faith is energized by love.[7] So a Spirit-directed life is a faith-filled life, demonstrating God's love to the world and being evidenced by these wonderful fruit in our lives.

Other Ways of Bearing Spiritual Fruit
Praising and Thanking God

*Therefore by Him let us continually offer the sacrifice of praise to God, that is, the **fruit of our lips**, giving thanks to His name. (Hebrews 13:15 NKJV)*

When we lift our voices in praise to God, it is an offering of fruit from our lips to Him.

Discipling Others

*I want you to know, dear brothers and sisters, that I planned many times to visit you, but I was prevented until now. **I want to work among you and see spiritual fruit**, just as I have seen among other Gentiles. (Romans 1:13)*

The fruit of the righteous is a tree of life, And he who wins souls is wise. (Proverbs 11:30 NKJV)

Sharing Financially What God Has Blessed Us With

*Therefore, when I have performed this and **have sealed to them this fruit**, I shall go by way of you to Spain. (Romans 15:28 NKJV)*

This verse refers to when Paul received an offering from the Gentiles for the poor believers in Jerusalem who were in need. He refers to their financial giving as "fruit."

When we invest financially into God's Kingdom work through our tithes and offerings, it results in fruit abounding in our lives.

*Not that I seek the gift, but I seek the **fruit that abounds to your account**. (Philippians 4:17 NKJV)*

What is The Purpose of Fruit?

Fruit provides us with both nourishment and seeds. We eat the flesh of the fruit for energy and sustenance. The seeds can be planted. Some seeds get cast away and don't find fertile soil, so they wither and die. Others find good soil and are able to grow and blossom into a new plant. These plants can then be nurtured and cared for, and when they reach maturity, will begin to produce fruit of their own.

Similarly, the spiritual fruit in our lives is there for others to see and be nourished by. Ultimately some will go on to produce fruit of their own.

Growing Spiritual Fruit Takes Time

Christians often get impatient when they don't see the spiritual fruit in their lives they would like to. An important thing to remember about spiritual fruit is that it takes time. If I sat outside expecting to watch an apple grow on a tree, I would sit for a long, long time before seeing a noticeable difference. If I planted an apple seed on Monday, it would be foolish to think I could enjoy homemade apple pie next week. Fruit takes time to grow to maturity.

The same is true spiritually. The growth we experience is rarely noticeable until much time has passed and we look back. Then we observe the growth and realize how we've changed.

Much of our Christian walk is about planting the seeds of faith in other people. This is done by the words we speak and the way we live. When we are joyful, peaceful, patient, and showing kindness, goodness and gentleness to others; when we exercise self-control over our sinful nature and love unconditionally, people take notice of our lives. They eat of our spiritual fruit and seeds of faith are planted in their hearts. As in nature, those seeds may or may not find fertile soil. Those that do take root can eventually blossom into a new and healthy tree, one that is planted by a river and will not suffer from a drought.

This is what the LORD says: "Cursed are those who put their trust in mere humans, who rely on human strength and turn their hearts away from the LORD. They are like stunted shrubs in the desert, with no hope for the future. They will live in the barren wilderness, in an uninhabited salty land. But blessed are those who trust in the LORD and have made the LORD their hope and confidence. They are like trees planted along a riverbank, with roots that reach deep into the water. Such trees are not bothered by the heat or worried by long months of drought. Their leaves stay green, and they never stop producing fruit." (Jeremiah 17:5-8)

In the Old Testament, Jeremiah likened the man who trusts in God to a tree planted near a river. The river (the LORD) will provide for the tree (the man), giving him nourishment and sustenance even during hard times. The tree will not only live, but also thrive and bear fruit.

As we grow with God, the roots of our lives will run deep and be continually nourished by the fountain of living water, Jesus Christ.

Today, Jesus is our source of living water. He says in John 4:14:

But those who drink the water I give will never be thirsty again. It becomes a fresh, bubbling spring within them, giving them eternal life.

As we grow with God, the roots of our lives will run deep and be continually nourished by the fountain of living water, Jesus Christ. Even during seasons of heat or drought we need not become anxious or worried. We remain at peace, trusting in Him. Abiding in Him, our leaves stay green, and never stop producing fruit.

Bearing Good Spiritual Fruit is Becoming Like Jesus

All spiritual fruit, including peace, is grown as we each abide in the vine and develop a close relationship with the Master. In doing so our whole outlook on life, and our character gradually changes. We become more Christlike. His thoughts become our thoughts. His actions become our actions. His purposes become our own.

All spiritual fruit, including peace, is grown as we each abide in the vine and develop a close relationship with the Master.

We begin to fulfill the Great Commission (Matthew 28:18-20) by becoming like Christ to the world. No longer living by the old sinful nature, we now live by the Spirit, and in doing so bear fruit. Others will see and eat of our fruit, and seeds will be planted in their hearts. Throughout our lives we plant and nourish, helping others reach maturity in Christ and begin bearing spiritual fruit of their own.

*Then the way you live will always honor and please the Lord, and **your lives will produce every kind of good fruit**. All the while, you will grow as you learn to know God better and better. (Colossians 1:10)*

A Christian should bear much spiritual fruit, as he or she faithfully and joyfully lives in relationship with the Lord. As we plant and water the seeds of faith in others we must always remember that it is God's job to make those seeds grow, blossom, and bear His wonderful fruit.

CHAPTER 11

Saved to Serve

American economist John Kenneth Galbraith, in his memoirs, *A Life in Our Times*, illustrates the devotion of Emily Gloria Wilson, his family's housekeeper:

> It had been a wearying day, and we had to go on to a dinner. I asked Emily to hold all telephone messages while I had a nap. Shortly thereafter the phone rang. Lyndon Johnson was calling from the White House.
>
> "Get me Ken Galbraith. This is Lyndon Johnson."
> "He is sleeping, Mr. President. He said not to disturb him."
> "Well, wake him up. I want to talk to him."
> "No, Mr. President. I work for him, not you."
> When I called the President back, he could scarcely control his pleasure. "Tell that woman I want her here in the White House."[1]

Who Do You Work For?

Do you ever ask yourself this question? Are you as devoted as Emily Wilson in honoring your boss and doing as he or she asks? Aside from your career or "day job," what about your heavenly calling? Which is more important? What takes priority in your life? If you say Jesus Christ is Lord, is your heart seeking Him all the time—and will you do as He says? If not, how will you know what you are to do?

"I have many things to do today—I must go to work, and carry out my other responsibilities—but Lord, what do you want me to do today? Show me Your love and who I can serve . . ."

Jesus is our constant companion, partner, and best friend. He is also our boss! He yearns to work alongside us in all we do. Remember the yoke?[2] When we enter into His peaceful presence early in the day, won't we be better equipped to hear His voice and carry out His direction?

Jesus tells us we can't serve two masters—our hearts can't be consumed with the things of the world and God at the same time—and what is in our hearts flows from our mouths.

> *Your eye is a lamp that provides light for your body. When your eye is good, your whole body is filled with light. But when your eye is bad, your whole body is filled with darkness. And if the light you think you have is actually darkness, how deep that darkness is!* **No one can serve two masters.** *For you will hate one and love the other; you will be devoted to one and despise the other. You cannot serve both God and money. (Matthew 6:22-24)*

> *A good person produces good things from the treasury of a good heart, and an evil person produces evil things from the treasury of an evil heart.* **What you say flows from what is in your heart.** *(Luke 6:45)*

Saved to Serve

What is Your Calling?

Many people think that being "called" by God happens only to pastors, nuns, missionaries, and other church leaders. But God says every member of the body of Christ is called to serve. Serving doesn't save us. We're saved for serving. Carrying out our call to serve, we become Christ's hands and feet to a world in need.

Fulfilling Your Purpose

In Christ, we are made the righteousness of God.[3] A simple but insightful definition of righteousness is "right living"—living the way God intends. This surely includes carrying out the Master's work through loving service to others. The result of our righteous work is peace.

> *The work of righteousness will be peace, And the effect of righteousness, quietness and assurance forever. (Isaiah 32:17 NKJV)*

Christ came to earth to do two things: serve humanity, and glorify God.

> *For even the Son of Man came not to be served but to serve others and to give his life as a ransom for many. (Mark 10:45)*

> *Let your light so shine before men, that they may see your good works and glorify your Father in heaven. (Matthew 5:16 NKJV)*

We're not meant to live for ourselves. God created us to serve others and to bring glory to Him. Jesus shows us how. If we're still busy following only our own agendas, God's peace will elude us. We must each count the cost and make the decision to serve as Christ did.

Renowned missionary Mother Teresa beautifully summed up the heart of Christian life and service when she said:

*The fruit of silence is prayer. The fruit of prayer is faith. The fruit of faith is love. The fruit of love is service. **The fruit of service is peace.***[4]

Jesus Calls Us to Serve Others

At what has come to be known as "The Last Supper," Jesus gives us a tender and moving example of service when He washes the feet of His disciples. At that time, it was the duty of the lowliest servant to wash the feet of guests. This wasn't a custom used only at Passover or regular meals, but any time strangers or travelers came into a house with dirt on their feet. The poorest of the servants had the humbling duty of washing the feet of a stranger.

Yet here, in a startling act of humility and compassion, our Lord puts a towel around his waist, pours water into a basin, kneels down and starts washing the feet of the disciples, one by one.

You call me "Teacher" and "Lord," and you are right, because that's what I am. And since I, your Lord and Teacher, have washed your feet, you ought to wash each other's feet. I have given you an example to follow. Do as I have done to you. I tell you the truth, slaves are not

*greater than their master. Nor is the messenger more
important than the one who sends the message. Now that
you know these things, God will bless you for doing them.
(John 13:13-17)*

If Jesus can take on the duty of the lowliest servant and wash
the disciples' feet, should not we emulate this kind of heart when
we deal with people? When we serve our fellow man in the way
Jesus instructs, we are serving Him. The Lord further explains
this in Matthew:

*Then these righteous ones will reply, "Lord, when did we
ever see you hungry and feed you? Or thirsty and give you
something to drink? Or a stranger and show you
hospitality? Or naked and give you clothing? When did
we ever see you sick or in prison and visit you?" And the
King will say, "I tell you the truth, **when you did it to one
of the least of these my brothers and sisters, you were
doing it to me!**" (Matthew 25:37-40)*

Let's not forget Jesus' humble beginnings. He was born in a
stable to a poor family. He worked as a carpenter and lived an
unpretentious life. He asked fishermen, tax collectors, and those
deemed unimportant in society to be His followers. He hasn't
asked us to do anything He wasn't willing to do Himself.

Pastor and author Rick Warren says in his blog:

*There are three things you can do with your life: You can
waste it, you can spend it, or you can invest it. The best
use of your life is to invest your life in something that will
outlast it.[5]*

It is clear that service to others with a righteous heart is an investment. Very few people invest their lives in serving others, yet Jesus says those who do will learn what it means to really live.

Only those who [give] away their lives for my sake and for the sake of the good news will ever **know what it means to really live.** *(Mark 8:35 LB)*

Service, Not Status

In today's "me" culture, true service remains unpopular. Rick Warren explains:

The world defines greatness in terms of power, possessions, prestige, and position. If you can demand service from others, you've arrived. In our me-first culture, acting like a servant is not a popular concept. Jesus, however, measured greatness in terms of service, not status. God determines your greatness by how many people you serve, not how many people serve you. This is so contrary to the world's idea of greatness that we have a hard time understanding it, much less practicing it. The disciples argued about who deserved the most prominent position, and 2,000 years later, people still jockey for position and prominence.

Thousands of books have been written on leadership, but few on servanthood. Everyone wants to lead; no one wants to be a servant. We would rather be generals than privates. Even Christians want to be "servant-leaders," not just plain servants. But to be like Jesus is to be a servant. That's what he called himself.[6]

A woman preparing for childbirth sometimes seeks the help of a doula. The doula is a non-medical person who assists and encourages the woman throughout her pregnancy. A doula serves the expectant mother by providing continuous support before, during, and after delivery. Doula is from the feminine form of doulos[7]—the Greek term for "slave" used many places throughout the New Testament.

In the opening of the book of Romans, the apostle Paul is described as a "slave" or "bond-servant"—a doulos of Christ.[8] In Luke, Mary responded to the news of her mothering the Son of God by saying *"Behold [I am] the maidservant (doule) of the Lord! Let it be to me according to your word."*[9]

A slave is under the control of and takes orders from the master. To be a servant of God as Paul and Mary were, reminds us to whom we owe our allegiance. We no longer are the servants or slaves of sin, but of Christ who bought us with the price of His life. Thus, slavery to Christ is a good thing!

Cultivating a Life of Christlike Service

Before experiencing the life-changing power of God's grace through Christ, we often remain too dominated by our own hurts and ways to think much about others. As our relationship with God develops, our lives take on the "higher purpose" He calls us to.

But my life is worth nothing to me unless I use it for finishing the work assigned me by the Lord Jesus—the work of telling others the Good News about the wonderful grace of God. (Acts 20:24)

Anyone who wants to be my disciple must follow me, because my servants must be where I am. And the Father will honor anyone who serves me. (John 12:26)

I believe God cares about our heart to serve more than our actual deeds. He is the searcher of all hearts and sees our motives and intentions, even though at times we fall short and make mistakes.

Nothing can touch the peace in your heart when you know you are serving Christ as He is personally directing you.

Many wonderful Christians fall into the trap of doing everything the church asks them (and sometimes burning out), instead of asking the Lord how He wants them to serve.

Nothing can touch the peace in your heart when you know you are serving Christ as He is personally directing you. Our service to Christ gauges the depth of our relationship with Him. When we are in love with Jesus above all else, we'll carry out His call to serve others—specifically as He tells us—and in doing so, we're serving Him.

How to Have a Servant's Heart

Do you desire to carry out Christ's work in the world?

Ask God to give you a servant's heart. Spend time with the Master, the Lord Jesus Christ, and learn from Him. Relationship is the most important part of a servant's heart.

Let's explore some of the attributes of a true servant of Christ:

Servants Are Humble

Servants don't call attention to themselves. Rather than seeking recognition from others for their good deeds, their hearts rest peacefully in the knowledge that they are pleasing the Lord. If recognized for their work they quietly accept it, but don't let it distract them from serving. The servant's heart stays humble.

Humility isn't denying your strengths; it's being honest about your weaknesses. Humble servants recognize that by themselves they can do nothing. Servants' strength comes from God alone. The Lord empowers their hearts with compassion, and whatever else is required to minister to those in need.

And all of you, serve each other in humility, for God opposes the proud but favors the humble. (1 Peter 5:5b)

True servants are content silently serving in the shadows, because they know that their reward in heaven is great. In one of his many writings, Andrew Murray beautifully describes the Christian heart of humility and the peace it brings to the soul:

Humility is perfect quietness of heart.** It is to expect nothing, to wonder at nothing that is done to me, to feel nothing done against me. It is to be at rest when nobody praises me, and when I am blamed or despised. It is to have a blessed home in the Lord, where I can go in and shut the door, and kneel to my Father in secret, and **am

*at peace as in a deep sea of calmness, when all around
and above is trouble.*[10]

Servants Are Compassionate

The heart of Christlike service is love.

*Instead, use your freedom to serve one another in love.
(Galatians 5:13b)*

Sympathy says, "I'm sorry you're hurt." Empathy says, "I
hurt with you." But compassion is saying "I'll do whatever I can
to stop your hurt."

Servants Encourage Others

Service includes making those around us better people by
our words and actions.

*So encourage each other and build each other up, just as
you are already doing. (1 Thessalonians 5:11)*

How often does a simple kind word brighten someone's day?
A word spoken at the right time from a heart of love can change
someone's life and give him or her the encouragement to keep
going when they're feeling ready to quit. Ask the Lord to give
you the words to speak that will minister grace to the hearers.[11]

Servants Are Not Selfish

Servants put other people ahead of themselves. Selfishness is
a stumbling block to serving others. The main reason we don't
have the time or energy to serve in the way Jesus asks is that
we're too preoccupied with our own plans and pleasures. Real

servants stay so focused on serving that they don't even think of themselves.

Don't look out only for your own interests, but take an interest in others, too. (Philippians 2:4)

*For you have been called to live in freedom, my brothers and sisters. **But don't use your freedom to satisfy your sinful nature**. (Galatians 5:13a)*

Servants are Ready and Willing

No soldier in active service entangles himself in the affairs of everyday life, so that he may please the one who enlisted him as a soldier. (2 Timothy 2:4 NASB)

A soldier is ready to jump into service whenever called upon—even at 2 a.m. Likewise, servants make themselves available to the Master and remain obedient to His call. They're ready to do what is needed, even when it's inconvenient. If we serve only when convenient, we don't have the true heart of a servant. We must be willing to surrender control of our own schedule and allow God to interrupt it when He needs to.

Servants see interruptions as divine appointments for ministry and rejoice at the opportunity to serve.

Servants let their Master set the agenda. They embrace interruptions as divine appointments for ministry and rejoice at the opportunity to serve.

Servants Help Others and Act Quickly

Servants pay attention to needs in others and look for ways to help. When God puts someone in need right in front of you, He's giving you the opportunity to serve. You must decide to seize the moment, or it's gone. Most of us can recall "missed opportunities" and the regret we felt afterward, especially if we're sure the Lord was prompting us to get involved.

We often get only one chance to help someone. If we pass it by, it may never return. We should have spiritual sensitivity and spontaneity, and be seeking opportunities to serve, so we can respond in love when they happen.

Therefore, whenever we have the opportunity, we should do good to everyone—especially to those in the family of faith. (Galatians 6:10)

Servants Don't Wait for Perfect Conditions

Servants don't procrastinate, make excuses, or wait for better circumstances. They do what needs to be done—*now*—not "when the time is right," or "one of these days."

Farmers who wait for perfect weather never plant. If they watch every cloud, they never harvest. (Ecclesiastes 11:4)

If you wait for perfect conditions, you will never get anything done.[12] Servants need to simply get busy serving. You may feel you don't have much to offer, but offer what you can. Ask the Lord for ways to serve and start doing what He directs. We learn and grow as we take action. Service is sometimes messy, and that's okay. Less-than-perfect service is always better than good intentions that never happen.

When someone comes to mind, it may be the Lord prompting you to pray for the person or reach out with a quick phone call or email. That simple act of obedience can make a huge difference in someone's life, often in ways we never see.

Servants Approach Every Task—Large or Small—With Love and Dedication

Work willingly at whatever you do, as though you were working for the Lord rather than for people. Remember that the Lord will give you an inheritance as your reward, and that the Master you are serving is Christ. (Colossians 3:23-24)

Don't wait for the "big" things to come along before serving. The little things are just as important and necessary. God will trust us with more when He sees our faithfulness to carry out the small things.

Jesus often carried out the mundane tasks that others avoided: washing feet, helping lepers, serving the sick. Nothing was beneath Him. It wasn't in spite of His greatness that He did these things but because of it. He tells us that whoever desires to be great must become a servant.

. . . but whoever desires to become great among you shall be your servant. (Mark 10:43b NKJV)

Those who are the greatest among you should take the lowest rank, and the leader should be like a servant. Who is more important, the one who sits at the table or the one who serves? The one who sits at the table, of course. *But not here! For I am among you as one who serves. (Luke 22:26b-27)*

We're never too important to help with small tasks. When done with love, they often yield the greatest opportunities for character building. In the little acts of service we become like Christ.

If you think you are too important to help someone, you are only fooling yourself. You are not that important. (Galatians 6:3)

Servants Are Reliable

Servants finish the job, keep their promises, and fulfill their responsibilities on time. They don't leave a task half done, nor do they quit when they get discouraged. Too often people make casual commitments and, without hesitation, break them for the slightest reason. If you say you will show up at 5:00, show up. If you say you're going to call someone, call. The servant keeps his or her word and is dependable and trustworthy. When faithful in the little things, God gives more.

If you are faithful in little things, you will be faithful in large ones. But if you are dishonest in little things, you won't be honest with greater responsibilities. And if you are untrustworthy about worldly wealth, who will trust you with the true riches of heaven? And if you are not faithful with other people's things, why should you be trusted with things of your own? (Luke 16:10-12)

Our reward for faithful service today is in eternity. Someday, standing before the judgment seat of Christ, we may hear these words:

> *The master said, "Well done, my good and faithful servant. You have been faithful in handling this small amount, so now I will give you many more responsibilities. Let's celebrate together!" (Matthew 25:23)*

A Life of Loving Service Fills Our Hearts With Peace

Years ago, in our small group home fellowship, someone remarked, "Serving others would be easy if it didn't involve people." Although we all laughed at the statement, it does reflect how we feel at times. When we grow tired of serving, we need to remember that we don't serve God by our own strength. He enables us to do what He's called us to do. When we're serving by the Lord's specific direction, peace fills our hearts and we don't run out of gas. Serving from our soul's convenience without His direction always drains our tank.

Whatever our talents, we're to use them to serve one another.

> ***God has given each of you a gift from his great variety of spiritual gifts. Use them well to serve one another.*** *Do you have the gift of speaking? Then speak as though God himself were speaking through you. Do you have the gift of helping others? Do it with all the strength and energy that God supplies. Then everything you do will bring glory to God through Jesus Christ. (1 Peter 4:10-11)*

The Christian life isn't about serving God instead of people. Serving others is serving God. Often in our enthusiasm to do God's work, we seek to become Bible scholars, but fail to do what it says, which includes helping the poor and hurting. It is too easy to go through the motions of being religious, but lack the loving service to others that Christ calls us to. Jesus saw this in the Pharisees in His day. They were busy with prayer, worship, and religious ritual, but in their zeal for serving God neglected the sick, the needy, and the sinner.

The Christian life isn't limited to the vertical. Those who readily lift their hands up, but don't stretch them out to help someone in need, are missing it. In contrast, those who serve without the revelation of how to do it will burn out doing merely good works.

How has your Christian service been lately? If it's not where you want it to be, or where you know it should be, ask God to help cultivate within you a servant's heart. Ask Him to make your heart His heart, and to show you how and where to serve. Get busy serving those around you, and you'll discover He will give you all you need—including His wonderful peace.

> *Those who readily lift their hands up, but don't stretch them out to help someone in need, are missing it.*

Father, fill our hearts with compassion that we may see others through your eyes; so we may reach out our hands in love to serve one another. Fill us with your peace as we carry out your work of righteousness. In the name of Jesus Christ, Amen.

CHAPTER 12

The Miraculous Mind of Christ

In a breakthrough once considered impossible, French scientists have accomplished a cross-species change of behavior by removing brain tissue from Japanese quail and implanting it in the brains of five chicken embryos. The transplant experiment worked. The hatched chicks sounded like quail instead of chickens![1]

Here's something even more amazing: God has "implanted" the mind of Christ in every person who accepts His Son as Savior. This is thrilling news! Through the Holy Spirit we now have a capacity for divine understanding that we never had before—enabling us to increasingly see and experience life from God's perspective. No academic degree or human achievement could accomplish this—only God's amazing gift of the Holy Spirit, freely given to us by His grace.

. . . for we have the mind of Christ. (1 Corinthians 2:16b)

Let this mind be in you which was also in Christ Jesus (Philippians 2:5 NKJV)

What Does it Mean to Have the Mind of Christ?

Is it simply to think good thoughts? Our minds don't always think pure and positive thoughts. Therefore, the mind of Christ cannot refer to our natural brain or the thinking in our head. There must be more to it. Let's examine the context of 1 Corinthians 2:16:

> "... No eye has seen, no ear has heard, and no mind has imagined what God has prepared for those who love him." But it was to us that God revealed these things by his Spirit. For his Spirit searches out everything and shows us God's deep secrets.

> **No one can know (oida) a person's thoughts except that person's own spirit, and no one can know (ginóskó) God's thoughts except God's own Spirit. And we have received God's Spirit (not the world's spirit), so we can know (oida) the wonderful things God has freely given us.**

> When we tell you these things, we do not use words that come from human wisdom. Instead, we speak words given to us by the Spirit, using the Spirit's words to explain spiritual truths. But people who aren't spiritual can't receive these truths from God's Spirit. It all sounds foolish to them and they can't understand it, for only those who are spiritual can understand what the Spirit means. Those who are spiritual can evaluate all things, but they themselves cannot be evaluated by others.

For, "Who can know the Lord's thoughts? Who knows enough to teach him?" But we understand these things, for we have the mind of Christ. (1 Corinthians 2:9-16)

Notice how much the Holy Spirit and the human spirit are mentioned in this section: "His Spirit," "person's own spirit," "God's own Spirit," "God's Spirit"(2x), "world's spirit," "the Spirit"(2x), and "those who are spiritual."

So what is Paul talking about? He is saying that spiritual discernment, or the ability to know something, is from God: "God revealed these things by His Spirit," "His Spirit searches out everything," "we can know the wonderful things God has freely given us," "only those who are spiritual can understand what the Spirit means," and "Who can know the Lord's thoughts?"

Receiving the Holy Spirit involves getting a "mind" we didn't have before that can understand and discern spiritual matters from God's perspective. This "mind of Christ" enables us to understand our identity in Christ, the Bible, God's love, spiritual discernment, direction, and anything else of God. It also enables us to recognize things from the devil.

In verses 11 and 12 (bolded) the word "know" is used three times. The first and third times use the Greek word *oida*, which refers to a seeing or knowing; a discernment, often referring to perceiving spiritually by revelation.[2] The purpose of the Spirit and the mind of Christ is that "we can **know** *(oida)* the wonderful things God has freely given us." The process of walking by the Spirit all begins with learning to hear or know *(oida)* the voice of the Lord. As we learn to live by His words, we then can **know** *(ginóskó*—to know by experience)[3] the things of God. This is significant! God clearly desires that we learn to live by the working of the Holy Spirit—hearing and obeying its instructions to us, so we might then experientially know Him.

> *To have the mind of Christ is the supernatural ability from the Holy Spirit to know in our spirit the things of God.*

At some point in our youth, many of us imagine what it might be like to someday have a child of our own. But not until we actually have a child do we start to really understand all it involves. What we heard about *(oida)* becomes a knowing by experience *(ginóskó)*. Similarly, by our own thoughts and reasoning we never really understand the depth, wisdom, and beauty of the things of God. Only by the working of Christ through the Holy Spirit do we first hear, and then experience these deeper spiritual truths and realities.

To have the mind of Christ is the supernatural ability from the Holy Spirit to know in our spirit the things of God.

Shouldn't we yearn to be in the Lord's presence that we might hear Him in the Spirit? Spiritually, we have the capability to understand and walk as Jesus did. By living in His presence, and hearing and obeying what He tells us, we experience more and more through the "mind of Christ." We become His hands and feet to the world.

The Mind of Christ vs. Our Natural Minds

Scripture makes it clear that our natural human minds cannot understand the way God works and thinks. So the mind of Christ doesn't mean that we know everything Christ does. In this age, *"we see things imperfectly, like puzzling reflections in a mirror."*[4]

"My thoughts are nothing like your thoughts," says the LORD. "And my ways are far beyond anything you could imagine. For just as the heavens are higher than the earth, so my ways are higher than your ways and my thoughts higher than your thoughts." (Isaiah 55:8-9)

No matter how much Bible we know, study, or memorize, we cannot begin to understand the way God works without His help. Through the speaking of the Spirit of Christ in us, we gain understanding of the things of God. The Holy Spirit shows us these things, and we begin to grasp how limitless and infinite God really is.

The mind of Christ allows us to:
- Think and act as Jesus does
- Submit to and follow His leading
- Do the Father's will, not our own
- Trust the Lord completely, instead of depending on our own understanding
- Make Christlike decisions

A Daily Choice

God lovingly designed the human mind to store knowledge, conceive ideas, use judgment, and exercise the power of reason. From it also emanates our will and emotions. As Christians, we choose every day to follow the leading of our own minds or the mind of Christ within us. God doesn't control us. From the beginning of time, He has given man the right to choose which way he will go.[5]

Today I have given you the choice between life and death, between blessings and curses. Now I call on heaven and earth to witness the choice you make. Oh, that you would choose life, so that you and your descendants might live! (Deuteronomy 30:19)

For the believer in Christ, the battlefield is in the mind. Words are the weapons used. The enemy attacks us with thoughts that come from words—words that at times come from people we love. Satan constantly lures us to see and perceive things from our own minds rather than by the mind of Christ.

These battles take place in two arenas: the "arena of faith" (the mind of Christ), and the "arena of unbelief" (our sinful nature). In the arena of faith we always win, but in the arena of our own mind we lose to the devil. The enemy knows this and shrewdly works to get us stuck in the arena of our sinful nature where doubt, unbelief, sin, and confusion enter in.

> *For the believer in Christ, the battlefield is in the mind. Words are the weapons used.*

When Jesus was on earth, He would often get away from everything to spend time alone with the Father in prayer.

After sending them home, he went up into the hills by himself to pray. Night fell while he was there alone. (Matthew 14:23)

. . . I tell you the truth, the Son can do nothing by himself. He does only what he sees the Father doing. Whatever the Father does, the Son also does. For the Father loves the

Son and shows him everything he is doing. (John 5:19-20a)

Jesus prayed, seeking the Father's mind and will for the things God wanted Him to do. We should do the same. We must spend time in the Lord's presence, silence our natural minds, and ask Him to help us clearly hear and see all the Father has for us, and wants to tell us.

How can we exercise the mind of Christ? A few suggestions are:

- When you read the Bible, ask God to supernaturally help you understand His truths with your spiritual mind, rather than relying on your natural mind for understanding.
- Spend time in prayer and communication with the Father. Ask God to reveal His will for you today.
- Learn to listen. Communication is a two-way street. Be silent, wait on the Lord, and receive whatever He has to tell you.
- Pay attention to the "impressions" you receive. Often they are God speaking to you in this "mind of Christ." (If they sound "off-key" to you, simply verify them from Scripture. What you hear from God will never contradict Scripture.)
- Write down in a journal what He tells you.

Some of the many benefits of living with the mind of Christ are:

- **Peace.** *"So letting your sinful nature control your mind leads to death. But letting the Spirit control your mind leads to life and peace." (Romans 8:6)*
- **Increased faith.** *"So then faith comes by hearing, and hearing by the word of God." (Romans 10:17 NKJV)*
- **Increased intimacy with the Lord.** *"Come now, and let us reason together," says the LORD . . ." (Isaiah 1:18a NKJV) "Now may the God of peace who brought up our Lord Jesus from the dead, that great Shepherd of the sheep . . . make you complete in every good work to do His will, working in you what is well pleasing in His sight, through Jesus Christ . . ." (Hebrews 13:20-21 NKJV)*
- **The treasures of wisdom and knowledge.** *"I want them to have complete confidence that they understand God's mysterious plan, which is Christ himself. In him lie hidden all the treasures of wisdom and knowledge." (Colossians 2:2b-3)*
- **Knowing God's will for our lives.** *" . . . may he equip you with all you need for doing his will. May he produce in you, through the power of Jesus Christ, every good thing that is pleasing to him." (Hebrews 13:21)*
- **The desire to live a life of obedience to Him.** *"Teach me your decrees, O LORD; I will keep them to the end. Give me understanding and I will obey your instructions; I will put them into practice with all my heart. Make me walk along the path of your commands, for that is where my happiness is found. Give me an eagerness for your laws rather than a love for money! Turn my eyes from worthless things, and give me life through your word." (Psalm 119:33-37)*

- **Keeping our lives anchored in the hope.** *"So think clearly and exercise self-control. Look forward to the gracious salvation that will come to you when Jesus Christ is revealed to the world."* (1 Peter 1:13)

Surely our minds and hearts can rest in peace more and more, as we learn to think and view life spiritually with the mind of Christ.

Now that we know the how and why of acquiring this new mind in Christ, we need to learn how to use it. In the next chapter we will explore the power of this new and amazing tool for our lives.

CHAPTER 13

Daily Transformation

To live with the mind of Christ is to think as He thinks. This doesn't come naturally! We have a sinful nature. The foundation of our lives—the kind of family we grew up in as well as our life experiences—shape our beliefs, ideas, paradigms, and perceptions of reality. If the people and experiences that influenced our thinking as children were godly, we'll find it easier to fix our thoughts on the things of God. If we were raised in dysfunctional, abusive conditions, we may struggle more with sinful thoughts and evil. *However, living with the mind of Christ clarifies any distorted thinking we may have.* Any believer can change!

Renewing the Mind

When we enter into relationship with God through Jesus Christ, we begin a process of *transformation.* We start thinking, feeling, and viewing things like God does. The Holy Spirit governs this process while teaching us the ways of Christ. What an exciting reality! To a great extent the depth and closeness of our relationship with Jesus Christ determines how much we will live like Him.

*And so, dear brothers and sisters, I plead with you to give your bodies to God because of all he has done for you. Let them be a living and holy sacrifice—the kind he will find acceptable. This is truly the way to worship him. Don't copy the behavior and customs of this world, but **let God transform you into a new person by changing the way you think**. Then you will learn to know God's will for you, which is good and pleasing and perfect. (Romans 12:1-2)*

The King James versions use the phrases "conformed" and "renewing the mind" in verse 2: "*. . . do not be **conformed** to this world, but be **transformed** by the **renewing of your mind**.*" To be conformed is to be fashioned after, or to follow a certain standard. We're not to follow the standards of the world, but instead we're to be transformed, which is to undergo a total change. This change happens in our minds as the Holy Spirit is at work.

It's worth taking a closer look at the word *transform*. A simple illustration of how it is used in nature offers us tremendous insight into this extraordinary process of transformation.

Caterpillar to Butterfly

In Romans 12:2 the Greek word translated "transform" is *metamorphóō*.[1] From it we get the word "metamorphosis," describing a complete change, like that of a caterpillar into a butterfly or a tadpole into a frog.[2] This change doesn't happen instantly, but takes place through various stages. In the case of the butterfly, first there is the egg, then the caterpillar (or larva), the chrysalis, and finally the butterfly.

Daily Transformation

Metamorphosis is a phenomenon of insects that is truly a biological miracle. It continues to amaze scientists. The caterpillar's mouth and digestive system are adapted for eating leaves. The butterfly's mouth is designed to suck nectar from flowers, and its digestive system suitable for the assimilation of honey. The caterpillar has scores of muscles, which are replaced by others of an entirely different structure in the butterfly. The caterpillar is earthbound, but when transformed it can fly. The contrast between caterpillar and butterfly is astonishingly remarkable and beautiful.

The process of metamorphosis beautifully illustrates the life of a Christian learning to walk in the steps of Christ.

The butterfly starts as an egg. It hatches and a tiny larva, or caterpillar emerges. The caterpillar ravenously eats leaves until it's fully-grown. As hormonal changes take place, it loses all interest in feeding. It spins a small silk pad on the underside of a leaf and hooks its little hind legs onto it. It begins to change and a hard shell, or chrysalis forms. During this stage, enzymes are released which literally digest all the caterpillar tissue and transform them into the structures of a butterfly. Finally, a butterfly emerges.

This intermediate state of chrysalis is a seeming death-like condition, in which the caterpillar actually dies for a time as it's changing, ending its previous way of living while preparing for its future existence as a butterfly.[3]

The process of metamorphosis beautifully illustrates the life of a Christian learning to walk in the steps of Christ. As we grow in Christ, the old sinful nature is being put to death while the "new nature" is being developed. Like the chrysalis stage, this is an extraordinary process that ends our previous ways of living and prepares us for new life in Christ. We literally go from a life of sin to living a Christlike life that glorifies God.

The Greek term *metamorphóō* is used only two other times in the New Testament. In 2 Corinthians it describes the same process from a different angle.

> *But we all, with unveiled face, beholding as in a mirror the glory of the Lord,* **are being transformed (*metamorphóō*) into the same image from glory to glory, just as by the Spirit of the Lord.** *(2 Corinthians 3:18 NKJV)*

Paul says that we are to take the veil (a reference to the sinful nature) away from our faces and behold the glory of the Lord. In doing so, we behold His glory as in a mirror, being *transformed* into the same image from (our) glory to (His) glory. This transformation is performed by the *Spirit of the Lord,* not us!

This wonderful transformation happens as we yield ourselves to the working of the Holy Spirit within us.

The third usage of *metamorphóō* is in Matthew 17:2, describing Jesus' transformation (transfiguration), when His face shone and His garments became white as light.

In Romans 12:2 we are not being told to renew our minds by our own effort. Our minds are being renewed. By whom? By the Holy Spirit. The chrysalis metamorphosis stage is a mystery to human understanding—how something can die and yet come back to life changed. So is the transforming process in Christ.

This wonderful transformation happens as we yield ourselves to the working of the Holy Spirit within us. In Colossians, Paul speaks of the riches and glory of Christ, saying *"And this is the secret: Christ lives in you. This gives you assurance of sharing his glory."[4]*

Daily we are being transformed by the renewing of our minds—rising up and changing as we die to ourselves and yield ourselves to Christ. More and more we become like Him, until our transformation is complete and perfected at His future appearing. At that time we will know as we are known, and receive new bodies like His. What a glorious day that will be!

Outward vs. Inward Transformation

Another Greek word is used in the New Testament for "transformed" with a different meaning. *Metaschematizo[5]* means "to transform by changing the outward appearance." Note its uses in 2 Corinthians 11:13-15 (NKJV):

*For such are false apostles, deceitful workers, **transforming** themselves into apostles of Christ. And no wonder! For Satan himself **transforms** himself into an angel of light. Therefore it is no great thing if his ministers also **transform** themselves into ministers of righteousness, whose end will be according to their works.*

The roots of the two Greek words *metamorphóō* and *metaschematizo* are quite different. *Morphe* lays stress on the inward change; while *schema* stresses the outward.[6] In the New Living Translation, the above passage uses the English word "disguise" instead of "transform."[7]

Satan wears a disguise to conceal his true identity. The devil's deceitful cohorts focus on changing the external, but cannot change the internal. God's focus is to transform the heart. As our inner being changes, the outer being follows. The Lord doesn't want us to wear a disguise and pretend to be changed. He wants us to truly change—be *transformed*—from the inside out. This can only happen with His help!

Religion, with its list of dos and don'ts, often causes people to wear a disguise of holiness and look like something they really are not. Many people act one way in church on Sunday, but are different people the rest of the week!

> *Only through an ongoing, intimate relationship with Jesus Christ are we transformed into His likeness.*

God wants to change your heart and soul, your thoughts and attitudes, your hopes and dreams to be like His. This change happens only from the inside out. While religion is all about outward appearances, true Christianity is about inner relationship. Only through an ongoing, intimate relationship with Jesus Christ are we transformed into His likeness.

Think Upon These Things

Moment by moment we choose what we think. We can't always stop bad thoughts from coming in, but we can decide what to do with them.

Fix your thoughts on what is true, and honorable, and right, and pure, and lovely, and admirable. Think about things that are excellent and worthy of praise. (Philippians 4:8)

Think about the things of heaven, not the things of earth
. . . for you have stripped off your old sinful nature and all
its wicked deeds. Put on your new nature, and be renewed
as you learn to know your Creator and become like him.
(Colossians 3:2, 9b-10)

As we yield ourselves to the new nature in Christ, He brings His truths to our minds as we need them. The Holy Spirit is renewing our minds while transforming us to become more and more like Christ.

Instead, let the Spirit renew your thoughts and attitudes.
(Ephesians 4:23)

How Did Peter Walk on Water?

When our focus is wholly on Jesus, we do the things that are pleasing in God's sight. Through Christ's strength the impossible becomes possible.[8]

Most people know that Jesus walked on water. But did you know that Peter did also? Let's look at the record:

Immediately after this, Jesus insisted that his disciples get
back into the boat and cross to the other side of the lake,
while he sent the people home. After sending them home,
he went up into the hills by himself to pray. Night fell
while he was there alone.

Meanwhile, the disciples were in trouble far away from
land, for a strong wind had risen, and they were fighting
heavy waves. About three o'clock in the morning Jesus
came toward them, walking on the water. When the

disciples saw him walking on the water, they were terrified. In their fear, they cried out, "It's a ghost!"

But Jesus spoke to them at once. "Don't be afraid," he said. "Take courage. I am here!" Then Peter called to him, "Lord, if it's really you, tell me to come to you, walking on the water." "Yes, come," Jesus said. So Peter went over the side of the boat and walked on the water toward Jesus. But when he saw the strong wind and the waves, he was terrified and began to sink.

"Save me, Lord!" he shouted. Jesus immediately reached out and grabbed him. "You have so little faith," Jesus said. "Why did you doubt me?" When they climbed back into the boat, the wind stopped. Then the disciples worshiped him. "You really are the Son of God!" they exclaimed. (Matthew 14:22-33)

How was Peter able to walk on the water? He had the "mind of Christ" with his focus one hundred percent on Jesus. But then along came the enemy who got Peter to look at the wind and the waves and succumb to fear. When Peter did, he began to sink.

The same happens to you and me. The devil tries to get our focus off the Lord so that we stumble and fall. When our hearts and minds are unwaveringly focused on Christ, He will help us carry out His work in the world—even if it means walking on water!

Daily Transformation

Keeping Us in Perfect Peace

God promises to guard our hearts and minds with His peace as we live in Christ Jesus. When something is guarded, it is protected.

His peace will guard your hearts and minds as you live in Christ Jesus. (Philippians 4:7b)

The process of dying to self and becoming like Christ happens daily as we choose to spend time with Him—to meet Him in that secret place, acknowledge His presence, walk and talk with Him. To live with the mind of Christ in the sweetness of His fellowship.

Gradually we are being transformed into His likeness. And in this amazing process, our hearts are guarded and kept in His perfect peace.

You will keep in perfect peace all who trust in you, all whose thoughts are fixed on you! (Isaiah 26:3)

CHAPTER 14

Internalizing Truth

Elizabeth Poland had no idea how severe the situation was as she sat on a bench at a caravan park on New Zealand's South Island. What started as a routine morning now found her sitting tensely all day, alone. Police checked in with her periodically to tell her how the search and rescue efforts for her husband were going. Elizabeth didn't know where her husband was or what state he was in, but something had happened. The experienced hiker had failed to return from a three-day trek around the mountainous Lake Adelaide region on the island.

As she waited and tried to ward off fear and apprehension, God spoke powerfully to her words of comfort she had memorized from the Psalms. (She had no Bible with her.) One Psalm especially ministered to her as the words flowed through her mind.

O LORD, you have examined my heart and know everything about me. You know when I sit down or stand up. You know my thoughts even when I'm far away. You see me when I travel and when I rest at home. You know everything I do . . . I can never escape from your Spirit! I can never get away from your presence! . . . How precious are your thoughts about me, O God. They cannot be numbered! I can't even count them; they outnumber the grains of sand! And when I wake up, you are still with me! . . . Search me, O God, and know my heart; test me and know my anxious thoughts. Point out anything in me that offends you, and lead me along the path of everlasting life. (Psalm 139:1-3, 7, 17-18, 23-24)

Later that day, Elizabeth found out it was no longer a search and rescue mission but a body retrieval. Her husband of 23 years had died after falling off a remote mountain cliff. "But God knew where he was. He had ordained his days," she later said.

Elizabeth shared how the comfort of that Psalm carried her through that dreadful day. The power of knowing Scripture by memory became evident again later that day as she found out the policeman in charge was also a Christian.

"In the middle of the night, with a full moon rising, he drove me back to where my children were, and as he did, he quoted Psalm 121," she said.

I look up to the mountains—does my help come from there? My help comes from the LORD, who made heaven and earth! . . . The LORD keeps you from all harm and watches over your life. The LORD keeps watch over you as you come and go, both now and forever. (Psalm 121:1-2, 7-8)

"Tears streamed down my face, and continue to flow, but God spoke powerfully to me that day and continues to do so," she said. "So yes, it [memorizing Scripture] seems like effort . . . but the benefits outweigh the effort!"[1]

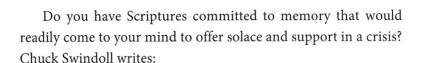

Do you have Scriptures committed to memory that would readily come to your mind to offer solace and support in a crisis? Chuck Swindoll writes:

*I know of no other single practice in the Christian life more rewarding, practically speaking, than **Scripture memorization** . . . **No other single exercise pays greater spiritual dividends!** Your prayer life will be strengthened. Your witnessing will be sharper and much more effective. Your attitudes and outlook will begin to change. Your mind will become alert and observant. Your confidence and assurance will be enhanced. Your faith will be solidified.*[2]

Most of us answer without hesitation when asked for our name, phone number, birthdate, or email address. That information is important to who we are, and we have committed it to memory. If asked what the Bible says about peace, does Romans 5:1 or Isaiah 26:3 come to mind as readily?

> *Memorizing Scripture is an important practical tool to help develop our spiritual lives.*

Memorizing Scripture is an important practical tool to help develop our spiritual lives. Before exploring it further, let's consider how we view God's Word.

Our Most Priceless Treasure

Have you ever been arrested for carrying your Bible to a

church service? For reading it in a restaurant or airport? For witnessing to the cashier at the supermarket? For inviting neighbors to a Bible study? For handing out tracts to strangers? If you live in America, you probably have not. We can openly carry and read our Bibles anywhere. We can own multiple Bibles and freely display them in our homes. Yet even with these freedoms (that are mostly taken for granted), how many dusty Bibles sit upon bookshelves in homes all across the United States? How many people allow entertainment, sports, electronics, and the media to fill their precious time?

> *If God's peace is deeply rooted in our hearts, it will be there when the crisis hits.*

In many parts of the world today, millions of Christians are still being persecuted and do not have Bibles to read. When facing trials, they cannot simply open God's Word to a favorite passage to find comfort. What would it be like to have your home searched and your Bibles confiscated? Or to sit in a prison cell for weeks without the Scriptures at your fingertips?

Praise God for the availability of His written Word! May we never take our Bibles for granted, but immerse ourselves in them daily.

Your laws are my treasure; they are my heart's delight. (Psalm 119:111)

Do you value the Word of God as a priceless treasure? Do you take your greatest delight in it? Do you hunger daily for God's words as you do for physical food? The Bible should be our most prized possession, for its words give us life!

Why Memorize Scripture?

When the unexpected event or crisis comes, as it did for Elizabeth Poland, it is said that true character emerges. If God's peace is deeply rooted in our hearts, it will be there when the crisis hits. If the Lord's presence is closer than our breath, we will immediately know He is with us and will see us through with all we need. If we have memorized verses that are meaningful and life-giving to us, they will come to mind when we need them to give us strength and comfort. We may not always have our Bibles in hand, but God's Word can be in our hearts and minds.

Those who love your instructions have great peace . . .
(Psalm 119:165)

Memorizing words that are important and meaningful allows us to internalize them and reflect on them deeply. They become part of who we are.

In the article "The Benefits of Memorizing Scripture," writer Danielle Marois says:

The perceived value of memorizing scripture, or of memorizing anything for that matter, has fallen on hard times in recent years. Trends in education, and the pervasive belief that memorization is simply a rote practice that has no real impact on true learning, have relegated memorization to an outdated, dusty tool. However, in dismissing the value of memorization, we have lost the practice of internalizing things that are worth keeping and pondering.

Isn't this the truth? With information literally at our fingertips through accessing the Internet, doesn't it become all too easy to say "If I need to know 'such and such,' I can just look it up online." Marois continues:

> *Memorizing words that are important and meaningful allows us to internalize them and reflect on them deeply.*

Memorization, whether of poetry, a favorite quote or of Scripture, allows you to reflect on the meaning of words repeatedly and in depth. The ultimate goal of memorization is not to regurgitate a thought for the sake of that accomplishment alone, but to allow the words to affect your thinking and your perspective. People who memorize poetry tend to do so because the words carry a message that resonates with them. 2 Timothy 3:16 tells us that all Scripture is divinely inspired and useful, so it is particularly beneficial to be able to recall passages from the Bible and allow those words to resonate.

Jesus used the Scripture He had memorized to refute the devil, and countless Christians have been strengthened and encouraged by the words of Scripture that have been brought to the forefront of their minds in difficult and perplexing times. What tool could be better to have at your fingertips? As people of God, we need to be intimately familiar with His words so that our perspectives can be aligned with His.[3]

Internalizing Truth

The Word of God is filled with exhortations to implant His truth in our hearts.

The law of his God is in his heart; None of his steps shall slide. (Psalm 37:31 NKJV)

How can a young person stay pure? By obeying your word. I have tried hard to find you—don't let me wander from your commands. I have hidden your word in my heart, that I might not sin against you. (Psalm 119:9-11)

For it is good to keep these sayings in your heart and always ready on your lips. (Proverbs 22:18)

The Benefits of Memorizing Scripture
Some key benefits gained from memorizing Scripture:

- **Helps you overcome worry and be at peace.** (Philippians 4:6-7)
- **Opens your heart to more intimate fellowship with Jesus Christ.** (1 John 1:3)
- **Follows the example of Jesus in resisting the devil.** Jesus quoted Scripture to the devil when confronted with temptation. He said out loud, "The Scriptures say" or "It is written . . . (insert verse)." (Matthew 4:1-10)
- **Gives you victory over sin.** (Psalm 119:9-11)
- **Sharpens you in the spiritual battle.** (Ephesians 6:12)
- **Provides wise counsel.** It gives you guidance, guards your thinking from error, and helps you make wise decisions. (Psalm 119:24, 105)

- **Equips you and gives you confidence to share your faith with others.** It also helps you counsel or minister to someone when your Bible is not on hand. (Colossians 3:16)
- **Produces spiritual growth and stability.** (Psalm 37:31)
- **Comforts you when you're sad.** It also equips you to comfort others. (2 Corinthians 1:4)

In her blog *A Holy Experience*, writer Ann Voskamp says:

What a heart knows by heart is what a heart knows . . . because when you are memorizing Scripture, quiet time with the Lord—becomes all the time.[4]

How to Memorize Scripture—Some Practical Tips

If you have never consciously worked on memorizing Scripture, don't be intimidated or think it's difficult. Our minds were designed to hold God's Word. His thoughts in our minds should be as natural as breathing. There is effort involved, but remember, you aren't doing this alone. The Lord is working with you!

There are many practical tips you can find for memorization. I will review some of the key ones and those that I've personally found beneficial. Find what works best for you. Memorizing Bible verses doesn't have to be another tedious task to fill your time. Instead, incorporate remembering and recalling Scripture into your daily routine. It then becomes simple—and even fun. Here are a few suggestions you may find helpful:

Internalizing Truth

To Begin Memorizing a Verse

- Choose a time when you're free from outside distractions.
- Talk to God about the verse and ask for His help in understanding it and committing it to memory.
- Read the verse in its context and in other Bible translations to gain more insight.
- Read the verse slowly and thoughtfully, silently and aloud.
- Each time you read it say the reference first, then the verse.

While Memorizing a Verse

- Say the Scripture reference, the verse, and then the reference again. (Knowing the reference is helpful if you forget the verse, and also if you want to show it to someone else in the Bible.)
- Break the verse into natural phrases. After learning the reference, learn the first phrase of the verse.
- Practice saying it out loud. Hearing yourself say the words helps reinforce them in your mind.
- Once you've repeated and learned the reference and the first phrase, continue adding phrases, one at a time. Repeat until you can quote the whole verse.
- Think about how the verse applies to your life.
- If memorizing a whole section or chapter, master one verse before moving onto the next.
- Use the verse in conversation as soon as possible.

129

After Memorizing a Verse

- Review it frequently in the following days. Repetition is the best way to keep it in your memory. Say it aloud, and use it in conversation.
- Writing the verse is helpful to deepen the impression in your mind.

Helpful Tools for Scripture Memorization

- **Free websites.** There are a number of websites specifically designed to help you learn Scripture. Search online to find the current resources.[5]
- **Apps.**[6] There are computer programs and smartphone apps available to help you memorize Bible verses.
- **Use flashcards.** Many people find it helpful to write the Scripture reference and topic on one side of a 3 x 5 card, and the Bible verse on the other. Carry the card with you throughout the day. Refer to it when you're standing on line in the grocery store, on your lunch break, or waiting for an appointment. Some people will use different color cards or markers to identify topics or books of the Bible.
- **Make a song.** Something special happens when words are set to music. Think of how many song lyrics you know simply from hearing the song over and over. When a melody comes to mind, so do the words! There are a number of websites with resources specifically designed to help you memorize Scriptures through song. Or, make up your own Scripture tunes.
- **Use gestures.** Make up hand movements to go with phrases. For example, Psalm 119:11: *"I have hidden your word in my heart, that I might not sin against you."* For

"I" point at yourself, make a gesture for "hidden," for "your" point upwards, for "word" make a gesture of a book, for "heart" bring hands together over your heart, and so on.

- **Make silly acronyms.** I remember learning Philippians 4:9 *"Keep putting into practice all you learned and received from me—everything you heard from me and saw me doing. Then the God of peace will be with you."* To remember the key words "learned," "received," "heard," and "saw," I memorized "Little Rock High School"—using the same first letters as Learned, Received, Heard, Saw.

- **Find a friend.** Ever find when you do things with someone else it becomes easier—and more fun? Find a friend who shares the goal of memorizing Scriptures, and practice and encourage each other.

Make Learning Scriptures Part of Your Daily Routine

Here's an example of how you might memorize Colossians 3:15 using some of the above mentioned techniques:

And let the peace that comes from Christ rule in your hearts. For as members of one body you are called to live in peace. And always be thankful.

Break the verse into natural phrases:
"And let the peace that comes from Christ"
"rule in your hearts."
"For as members of one body"
"you are called to live in peace."
"And always be thankful."

Take the first phrase and read it. Repeat it silently in your mind. Repeat it out loud. Write it down. Do this several times, and gradually add the next phrase, then the next. Follow the same process until you can repeat and write the entire verse.

Write the verse on cards and put them in places where you'll see them during your day—the bathroom mirror, in your closet, your dashboard, on your desk or computer screen, on the refrigerator, etc. Whenever you see the card, rehearse the verse in your mind.

Similarly, incorporate some of the other techniques mentioned into your daily routine. Make it fun. Before you know it you'll be able to recite many verses by heart.

What is Christian Meditation?

The story goes that Henry Ford once hired an efficiency expert to evaluate his company. After a few weeks, the expert made his report, which was highly favorable except for one thing.

Focused thinking often sparks great ideas and deep insights for those who take the time to ponder deeply.

"It's that man down the hall," said the expert. "Every time I go by his office he's just sitting there with his feet on his desk. He's wasting your money."

"That man," replied Mr. Ford, "once had an idea that saved us millions of dollars. At the time, I believe his feet were planted right where they are now."[7]

Focused thinking often sparks great ideas and deep insights for those who take the time to ponder deeply. For the Christian, great "aha" moments of understanding from the Holy Spirit often come after time is spent meditating on the things of God, a verse, or passage of Scripture. Christian meditation is a concept deeply rooted in the Word of God.

Unfortunately, in today's culture the word "meditation" often carries the connotation of something mystical. It's generally seen as a practice of the New Age movement because of its association with Transcendental Meditation (TM), which is steeped in Hindu philosophy. For some, meditation is communing with the spirit world around us. For others, it brings pictures of sitting in unusual positions while "clearing the mind." None of these depict Christian meditation.

Eastern meditation is characterized by self-centered objectives. It uses techniques like concentrating on objects, using "controlled" breathing, and uttering mantras—all with the purpose of emptying the mind of distractions. This then supposedly enables a person to reach a state of harmony with themselves and the universe. All of these techniques focus on *self-centered motives.*[8]

Biblical meditation has nothing to do with emptying our minds, or looking within ourselves for selfish reasons.

Many people innocently practice this kind of meditation with the goal of simple relaxation. Eastern meditation in any form is dangerous because it draws people away from God by encouraging them to look inwardly to themselves for peace and answers. The notion of emptying one's mind also opens up the availability of demonic deception, manipulation, and possession.

We must be careful, however, not to write off meditation simply because it is practiced by Eastern mystics.

Filling, Not Emptying

Biblical meditation has nothing to do with emptying our minds, or looking within ourselves for selfish reasons. Christian meditation centers on the relationship we have with God through Jesus Christ. It allows us to contemplate deeply God Himself, His creation, His Word, His faithfulness, and our relationship with Him. It invites our hearts and minds to fill with His wisdom, discernment, peace, and joy, as we look upward to God and outward to others. Christian meditation should engage every part of us, as author Joyce Huggett writes:

We meditate to give God's words the opportunity to penetrate, not just our minds, but our emotions—the places where we hurt—and our will—the place where we make choices and decisions. We meditate to encounter the Living Word, Jesus himself. We meditate so that every part of our being, our thoughts and our affections and our ambitions, are turned to face and honour and glorify him.[9]

The Word of God is central to Christian meditation because it is the place where our knowledge of God begins. As we meditate upon the words of God, we ask Him to give us understanding by the Holy Spirit, who promises to lead us into "all truth."[10]

In *Satisfy Your Soul*, Dr. Bruce Demarest writes:

A quieted heart is our best preparation for all this work of God . . . Meditation refocuses us from ourselves and from the world so that we reflect on God's Word, His nature,

His abilities, and His works . . . So we prayerfully ponder, muse, and "chew" the words of Scripture . . . The goal is simply to permit the Holy Spirit to activate the life-giving Word of God so that something more of our lives is transformed to bring us, every day, a little closer to the image of Christ.[11]

When Should We Meditate?

God tells us to meditate on His Word day and night.[12] Throughout the day we should be mindful of seeking His presence and drawing our thoughts to His words.

For most Christian believers there are at least three times during the day we should meditate on the things of God. Just before falling asleep, turn your thoughts to God to close the day. Upon awakening, let Him be your first thought as you praise Him for a new day and enter His presence. Lastly, find a specific time each day for reading the Bible and prayer. For many, the morning works well for this, as it helps us prepare our hearts to dwell in the Lord's presence, to converse with Him, and to hear His voice throughout the day.

Why Should We Meditate?

- **For understanding.** *"Think about what I am saying. The Lord will help you understand all these things."* (2 Timothy 2:7)
- **So our words and hearts might please God.** *"May the words of my mouth and the meditation of my heart be pleasing to you, O LORD, my rock and my redeemer."* (Psalm 19:14)
- **To obey God and find success and prosperity.** *"Study this Book of Instruction continually. Meditate on it day*

and night so you will be sure to obey everything written in it. Only then will you prosper and succeed in all you do." *(Joshua 1:8)*

What Should We Meditate On?

- **His Word.** *"I have more understanding than all my teachers, for Your testimonies are my meditation." (Psalm 119:99 NKJV) Also, Psalm 119:23,48 and Psalm 119:15,78,97,148 (NKJV)*
- **His love.** *"O God, we meditate on your unfailing love as we worship in your Temple." (Psalm 48:9)*
- **His works and mighty deeds.** *"I will also meditate on all Your work, And talk of Your deeds." (Psalm 77:12 NKJV) Also, Psalm 119:27; 143:5 (NKJV); 145:5.*

A few more things I can meditate on:
- **The things God has done in my life, or others**
- **The salvation He has freely given me**
- **The peace I have in Christ**
- **Something the Lord has taught me, or insights He has given me**
- **The life He has freed me from and my new life in Christ**
- **The holiness of God**
- **The faithfulness of God**
- **The brevity of our lives on this earth and what is coming in the future when the Lord returns**
- **The meaning or application of a specific passage of Scripture**

Becoming More Like Christ

Meditation can be a time of our greatest formation in Christ, as we contemplate deeply the things of God. During profound reflection the Lord often gives us "lightbulb" moments of insight and understanding. Perhaps you've experienced these exciting and reassuring times.

Meditation affords us time to richly relish our relationship with Him. We joyfully give thanks for all the Lord has done and is doing in our lives. We seek to understand and obey His words. We ponder new ways to serve Him.

Meditating on Scripture and memorizing Scripture go hand in hand. Often, as we meditate on a verse we begin to also commit it to memory. Both allow us to reflect upon and internalize what God is saying. As our digestive systems process the food we eat so it can be of use to our bodies, so meditation assimilates the things of God in our hearts so we can powerfully live for Him.

Meditation can be a time of our greatest formation in Christ, as we contemplate deeply the things of God.

We experience God's peace in profound and meaningful ways as we memorize His words and meditate upon them often.

~ Part Three ~

Living in the Lord's Presence

Peace is not the absence of trouble, but the presence of Christ.
~Sheila Walsh[1]

CHAPTER 15

Peace Under Pressure

Cornelius McGillicuddy, known as Connie Mack, was one of the longest-serving managers in Major League Baseball history, and one of the greats. He managed the Philadelphia Athletics for their first 50 seasons of play, from 1901-1950, when Mack retired at age 87. During his career, his team won nine American League pennants and five World Series.

In his first three years as a manager, Mack's teams finished sixth, seventh, and eighth. Losses consumed him, and he worried a lot. He took responsibility for the placements, and actually demoted himself back to the minor leagues to give himself more time to develop his leadership skills.

When he returned to the major leagues, he became so successful in handling his players that he eventually grew the best team the world had seen at the time.

Mack's strength was finding the best players, training them well, and simply letting them play. He understood that people were individuals and didn't believe that baseball revolved around managerial strategy. He learned how to lead and inspire his men.

Mack never criticized a player in front of others. He would

wait a day before discussing mistakes with players to give himself time to cool down emotionally. But Mack's biggest key to effective management was to not worry. Later in life he shared how worry had threatened to wreck his career early on. He saw how unproductive it was and started to force himself to get so busy preparing to win games that he had no time left to worry about the ones that were already lost.

> *For his 1944 book* How to Stop Worrying and Start Living, *Dale Carnegie asked Mack if he ever worried over games that were lost.* "Oh yes I used to," *Mack was quoted.* "But I got over that foolishness long ago. I found out it didn't get me anywhere at all. You can't grind any grain with water that has already gone down the creek." *From that experience was born the philosophy he impressed on Connie, Jr.:* "Son, there is never a worry worth taking to bed with you. When you look back on any worry, you will always wonder why you took it so seriously in the first place."[1]

I don't know if Connie Mack was a Christian or not, but he had learned an important lesson for successful living. *There's no profit in worrying.* Jesus also cautions us that once we start making money, success, or things our primary focus, worrying about them is inevitable and often becomes all-consuming. After acquiring what we want, those things quickly lose their luster, as we're already preoccupied with getting something better or more. Enough is never enough.

> *That is why I tell you **not to worry about everyday life—whether you have enough food and drink, or enough***

clothes to wear. Isn't life more than food, and your body more than clothing? Look at the birds. They don't plant or harvest or store food in barns, for your heavenly Father feeds them. And aren't you far more valuable to him than they are? **Can all your worries add a single moment to your life?**

And **why worry about your clothing?** *Look at the lilies of the field and how they grow. They don't work or make their clothing, yet Solomon in all his glory was not dressed as beautifully as they are. And if God cares so wonderfully for wildflowers that are here today and thrown into the fire tomorrow, he will certainly care for you. Why do you have so little faith?*

So **don't worry about these things, saying, "What will we eat? What will we drink? What will we wear?"** *These things dominate the thoughts of unbelievers, but your heavenly Father already knows all your needs. Seek the Kingdom of God above all else, and live righteously, and he will give you everything you need.*

So **don't worry about tomorrow,** *for tomorrow will bring its own worries. Today's trouble is enough for today.* (Matthew 6:25-34)

Many people, including Christians, worry because they don't trust God's promise of providing the basic necessities of life. People stress over money because they feel they never have enough. They worry about making ends meet, living from paycheck to paycheck. People become consumed with possessions and then become stressed out maintaining all their "stuff." Many have believed the lie that owning things and having money relieve stress and lead to happiness and contentment.

When we've allowed the worries and stresses of life to fill our hearts with concern, they quickly squelch our trust in God. They make it difficult to hear the Lord's voice. They rob us of our peace.

There are two ways we can handle life's pressures—the world's way, or God's way. We choose.

Handling Life's Pressures—The World's Way

Have you ever felt overwhelmed by your circumstances? Overloaded with too much work to do? "Stressed out" is a common expression we hear. The close companions of doubt, worry, anxiety, and fear work together to cause us anguish. They challenge and threaten our well-being—emotionally and physically. We begin to wonder how we can cope with the pressures placed upon us.

Psychologists say that without stress our lives would be boring and probably feel pointless. Stress is a normal part of life and something we all experience. Not all stress is bad. Some stresses are good and get us moving. Short-term good stress, such as a job interview, an important presentation, hosting a party, performing on stage, or being in a sporting event, can give us the extra energy needed to perform our best.

God also designed us with a wonderful physiological response to certain stressors. Ever had a sudden scare or an unexpected crisis? When facing a challenge or a threat, our bodies' sympathetic nervous system goes to work, activating a fight-or-flight response to protect us. The body produces higher levels of the hormones cortisol and adrenaline, which trigger heightened alertness, heart rate, sweating, and muscle preparedness—all to protect us in dangerous or challenging situations. There are amazing stories of people who have lifted a tree or a car off someone trapped. It's incredible how God equips us to perform when needed!

God did not intend, however, that people remain in the "fight-or-flight" response long-term. Yet for many, it becomes a lifestyle because they're unable to manage their stress. Being in high-alert mode for long periods of time inevitably impacts physical health and is the cause of much sickness and disease.

When such stress lingers and begins to undermine our mental and physical health, it is bad stress. Today's fast-paced, hectic lifestyle lends itself to uncertainty and anxiety. If left unchecked, it begins to affect our health in powerful ways. One day our bodies signal us that something is wrong, and we wonder "where did that come from?"

The pressures of today's world are constantly bearing down on us. Our political leaders have led our children, our grandchildren, and us into tremendous debt. The value of retirement assets is dropping. People are losing their homes through foreclosure or violent weather. The unemployment rate remains high. All around the globe the challenges are similar. The world is a volatile and unpeaceful place.

Negative stress is inevitable, but how we deal with it is our choice, and has a huge impact not only on our physical health but also on our emotions, our behavior—and our peace of mind. Common causes of stress and worry are:
- Relationships
- Family problems
- Daily needs: food, rent, bills

- Losing a loved one
- Finances, interest rates, the stock market
- Sickness and health
- Job issues
- Moving to a new home
- Lack of time

Other kinds of stress include:
- Pregnancy, miscarriage
- Abortion
- Becoming a parent
- Losing a job
- Divorce
- Conflicts in the workplace
- Driving in heavy traffic
- Noisy neighbors
- Uncertainty (i.e., waiting for results of medical tests, college applications, exams, or job interviews)
- Pleasing people

Common methods of stress management include exercise, good nutrition, controlling alcohol and caffeine use, deep breathing, talking to others, relaxation techniques such as massage or quiet music, and learning to say no—all good things to incorporate into our lives.

Some people follow the route of addictions to cope with stress. Over-drinking, over-eating, over-shopping, over-spending, and over-working are commonplace in our culture. Others who can't get a handle on managing stress fall into a deep mental darkness and depression. They surrender to thoughts of worthlessness, hopelessness, and even suicide.

Worldly advice to combat stress and worry often goes like this: *"Just think positive! . . . Don't worry—it may never happen! . . . You're in charge, get control of yourself. . . . Get busy doing things to take your mind off your problems. . . . It will be over soon. . . . This too shall pass. . . . Just stop worrying! . . . Go see a therapist. . . . Have another drink. . . . This is just the 'cross you have to bear.' . . . Laugh your troubles away."* And of course, the classic advice of the song, *"Don't worry—be happy!"*

The only true starting point for managing stress is Jesus Christ.

However, all the self-discipline in the world still doesn't eliminate stress and produce lasting peace. The only true starting point for managing stress is Jesus Christ. A life apart from Him makes dealing with stress a debilitating and often impossible task.

Handling Life's Pressures—God's Way

Why not change the words to the song: *"Don't worry—be peaceful!"*

But is peace really as simple as telling myself to be peaceful?

Philippians 4:6-7 is a familiar passage in which God tells us not to worry, and what to do instead to experience peace:

Don't worry about anything; instead, pray about everything. Tell God what you need, and thank him for all he has done. Then you will experience God's peace, which exceeds anything we can understand. His peace will guard your hearts and minds as you live in Christ Jesus.

The word "worry" is an interesting and revealing study. Let's explore these verses in Philippians more closely:

Don't worry about anything . . .

The Greek verb used for worry is *merimnao*—etymologically derived from *merizo* = "to divide" and *nous* = "mind." *Merimnao* is defined as "to be anxious, or troubled with cares."[2] Isn't our mind divided when we're anxious? Can we be trusting God and worrying at the same time? Worrying can be thought of as a "dividing of the mind."

Don't worry about *anything*? Can He really mean ANY THING? That's what it says!

It's interesting that *merimnao* is also used five times as "worry" in the latter part of Matthew 6, which we read earlier.

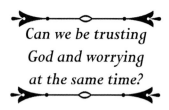

Can we be trusting God and worrying at the same time?

" . . . *I tell you not to worry about everyday life—whether you have enough food and drink, or enough clothes to wear." (vs. 25) "Can all your worries add a single moment to your life?" (vs. 27) "And why worry about your clothing?" (vs. 28) "So don't worry about these things, saying, 'What will we eat? What will we drink? What will we wear?" (vs. 31) "So don't worry about tomorrow . . . " (vs. 34)*

God's will is clearly that we do not worry—ever! Our minds are not to be divided between worrying about our need and trusting in His promised provision. We cannot be living in the unbelief of worry and the belief of faith at the same time.

"Give all your worries . . . to God, for he cares about you." [3]

. . . instead, pray about everything.

Prayer is a key ingredient to living in God's peace. However, if our prayer life is no more than presenting God our shopping list of things we want or need, it may be challenging to allow His peace to guard our hearts.

If you're a parent, do you like it if your son or daughter only talks to you to tell you what he or she needs? Don't some of the most gratifying moments of relationship come through discussion, a word of thanks, saying "I love you," or an acknowledgment of trust?

God wants us to go to Him with everything.

Tell God what you need . . .

If we're to go to God with everything, it surely means we're talking to Him more than once or twice a day. No need is too great or too small for Him to hear and care for. Good relationship requires dialogue, not just monologue. Prayer isn't only about us talking to God, but also about Him talking to us. We must take time to listen.

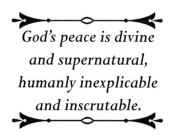

God's peace is divine and supernatural, humanly inexplicable and inscrutable.

. . . and thank Him for all He has done.

In addition to telling Him what we need, we should spend time thanking Him for all He's done. Don't thanks and praise bring our minds to a place of trust and faith better than worry or fear?

Then you will experience God's peace . . .

"Then"—only after not worrying about anything, praying about everything, and thanking Him, will we experience God's peace.

. . . which exceeds anything we can understand.

God's peace passes all understanding.[4] The peace found in Jesus Christ is unlike anything the world can offer. Remember Jesus' words in John 14:27:

> I am leaving you with a gift—peace of mind and heart. And the peace I give is a gift the world cannot give. So don't be troubled or afraid.

The peace of God defies all understanding. It transcends the faculty of the mind. God's peace is divine and supernatural, humanly inexplicable and inscrutable. Psychology cannot explain it, yet a believer in relationship with Jesus Christ can experience it.

His peace will guard your hearts and minds . . .

The peace of God patrols before the heart's door, like a sentinel, defending it from attacks of anxiety, fear, and temptation.

"Guard" in the Greek is a military term meaning a mounted guard, standing post at the entrance to a city. The city of Philippi was a military outpost of the Roman government. Soldiers were on duty, guarding the city gate from within.

What will the peace of God guard? Our hearts and minds. The use of future tense here assures us results. The peace of God patrols before the heart's door, like a sentinel, defending it from attacks of anxiety, fear, and temptation.

. . . as you live in Christ Jesus.

For those living a walk of faith, peace should be the norm. After all, the Prince of Peace is in us! Communion with Christ is our domain for peace. As we grow in relationship with Him, we will live with God's perfect peace guarding our hearts and minds more and more.

Why not take a moment right now to thank the Lord for His presence and peace?

Developing a Christian Attitude Toward Worry and Stress

Many times the root of negative stress and anxiety is fear.

An acronym for fear is False Evidence Appearing Real. Fear is ugly. Fear masks truth. The truth for Christians is that God loves us, is with us, and promises to supply our need. When we're not focused on truth, it's easy to end up worrying. His Word tells us God is not the author of fear,[5] and there is no fear in love.[6]

God didn't design us to hold fear, but faith. We were fashioned for faith! When trustfully resting in His presence, fear dissipates.

Theologian Dr. E. Stanley Jones writes:

I am inwardly fashioned for faith, not for fear. Fear is not my native land; faith is. I am so made that worry and anxiety are sand in the machinery of life; faith is the oil. I live better by faith and confidence than by fear, doubt and anxiety. In anxiety and worry, my being is gasping for breath—these are not my native air. But in faith and confidence, I breathe freely—these are my native air. A

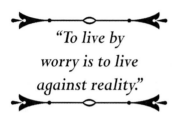

"To live by worry is to live against reality."

John Hopkins University doctor says, "We do not know why it is that worriers die sooner than the non-worriers, but that is a fact." But I, who am simple of mind, think I know; We are inwardly constructed in nerve and tissue, brain cell and soul, for faith and not for fear. God made us that way. To live by worry is to live against reality.[7]

Worrying is contrary to the attitudes God desires for us. Worrying is unbelief. Unbelief is sin. Rather than worry, we're to look to God in our situation.

Give your burdens to the LORD, and he will take care of you. He will not permit the godly to slip and fall. (Psalm 55:22)

The Christian response to worry is not to seek escape or removal from our problems. Rather, we're to diligently seek God in our stresses and trials, trust in Him, offer prayers of faith, and find encouragement in His Word and His presence. Instead of disquieting worry, the result will be comfort and peace.

In the multitude of my anxieties within me, Your comforts delight my soul. (Psalm 94:19 NKJV)

Worry weighs a person down; an encouraging word cheers a person up. (Proverbs 12:25)

Peace Under Pressure

O my people, trust in him at all times. Pour out your heart to him, for God is our refuge. (Psalm 62:8)

Sinful behaviors, including unforgiveness, are often the cause of much stress in our lives. They rob us of the peace God desires for us to have.

The biblical remedy for sin is repentance and forgiveness. Ephesians exhorts us not to give place to the devil through sin.[8] To give place is to grant legal right to. We give satan entrance into our lives through sin. We cancel his authority over us through repentance and forgiveness.

God wants everyone to repent.[9] To repent is to change. With godly sorrow, go to the Father and ask forgiveness for believing the lie of the enemy over His truth. Thank Him for releasing you from the stronghold of the lie of sin. Then ask Him to reveal His truth to you about the situation.

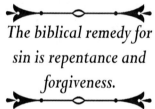

The biblical remedy for sin is repentance and forgiveness.

Take time to listen after you pray. Likewise, ask for forgiveness, and forgive others also. To forgive is not to condone the wrongs committed against you. But forgiving those who wronged you releases satan's grip on you in that wrong. It's always your choice to forgive. Doing so eliminates much unwanted and often underlying stress in life, and makes room for God's peace to replace it.

Jesus reminds us that we will have trials and sorrows here on earth, but to take heart, because He has overcome the world. In Him there is peace.[10] The apostle Paul says our present troubles are temporary. "Present troubles"[11] or "light affliction"[12] is also translated elsewhere as "tribulation"—or in the vernacular "mental pressure."

> *For our present troubles are small and won't last very long. Yet they produce for us a glory that vastly outweighs them and will last forever! So we don't look at the troubles we can see now; rather, we fix our gaze on things that cannot be seen. For the things we see now will soon be gone, but the things we cannot see will last forever. (2 Corinthians 4:17-18)*

From a godly perspective our present troubles are small and short in duration in light of future realities. Therefore, we need to keep our focus not on what we see now but on what is unseen and lies ahead.

How Jesus Handled Stress

Jesus handled everything, including stress, by saying and doing only what the Father told Him.

> *I don't speak on my own authority. The Father who sent me has commanded me what to say and how to say it. (John 12:49)*

> *I tell you the truth, the Son can do nothing by himself. He does only what he sees the Father doing. Whatever the Father does, the Son also does. (John 5:19)*

How would our lives change if we said and did only what the Lord told us? If He truly is our partner, our yokefellow, our friend, we can and should confer with Him before doing anything. Wouldn't the Prince of Peace be able to help you handle the stress in your life? Take comfort. He can and He will. Right now. He is with you and in you.

Surely, as Jesus hung on the cross He experienced the ultimate stress. His head was crowned with thorns, His hands and feet pierced with nails, His face bruised, His back shredded. People on the ground cruelly shouted insults at Him. His closest companions deserted Him. He carried the burden of the sins of the world upon Himself.

Yet even in the midst of this unfathomable stress, His response to it flowed from His unwavering faith in the Father. Through the Spirit's empowering He was able to say, *"Father, forgive them, for they don't know what they are doing."* [13]

How would our lives change if we said and did only what the Lord told us?

We are to handle stress in our lives the same way. Christ dwells in us! Through the enabling of the Holy Spirit and living by Christ's personal *rhema* instructions to us, we can carry the peace of God in any situation. In the midst of the doubt, worry, fear, and stress that daily threaten to consume us, we experience Christ's victory as we dwell in His peaceful presence.

And let the peace that comes from Christ rule in your hearts. For as members of one body you are called to live in peace. And always be thankful. (Colossians 3:15)

155

CHAPTER 16

The Quiet Classroom

Growing up during the emergence of rock and roll, music was a big part of my life. Each year during Christmas break from school, as the old year was coming to a close and a new year beginning, the big radio station out of New York City would play the "Top 100" hits of the year for a week. I would be glued to the radio, trying to log a complete list of all 100 songs. Not only that, but I could usually sing along to every song, word for word!

As a kid, I had a huge music collection and would pretend to be a singer, lip-syncing to songs with a make-believe microphone. My dream was to be a "backup singer," one of the girls who stood behind the lead singer, swaying gently and supplying harmonies.

My voice wasn't the greatest, but I could dream, right?

As the years went on my love for music grew. I took piano lessons and practiced every day. I started ice skating, and loved to glide along the ice to the music at the rink.

I listened to music constantly. As soon as I was home, music went on; the minute I got into the car, the radio flipped on. At friends' houses we loudly cranked the current songs and had dance marathons. It got to the place that I never had a moment of silence. I always had a song going in my head. In short, *I was addicted to music!*

In the midst of my teenage years when I became a Christian, I started to learn the importance of spending time in Bible reading and prayer. I learned that what I choose to fill my mind with makes a difference in what I think and how I live. To cultivate the qualities of a Christlike life requires deliberate decisions and actions. I realized certain old habits would have to change and new ones be developed to take their place. I also realized I didn't know how to be quiet on the inside!

Now you may be thinking there are certainly worse things to be addicted to than music. I don't disagree. But the point is— what do you spend most of your time thinking about? Do your thoughts race, obsess, or continually replay incidents or scenarios?

Are you comfortable with silence?

Sitting Quietly in a Room Alone

Greek philosopher and mathematician Pythagoras[1] wrote *"Learn to be silent. Let your quiet mind listen and absorb."*

Twenty-one centuries later French mathematician, physicist, and Christian apologist Blaise Pascal[2] said *"All man's miseries derive from not being able to sit quietly in a room alone."*

Pythagoras and Pascal were each considered great scientific minds during their time. It's interesting to note that as scientists, they both spoke of the importance of silence and the value of quiet meditation.

Their messages speak of a way of life not commonly sought after or encouraged in today's culture—that there is great profit in spending quiet time.

Most people's minds race full-tilt day and night. It's been estimated that the average person thinks 70,000 separate thoughts each day. Most are a jumble of continuous dialogue about ordinary daily "stuff": work, schedules, money concerns, grocery lists, sexual fantasies, vacation plans, children, and on and on. They create mental patterns that leave little room for silence.

These thought patterns support our cultural norm that all gaps, or silences in conversation should be quickly filled. Silence often represents an embarrassment or a social defect. When talk falls still at a dinner party, it's perceived as an awkward moment. Good conversationalists learn to swiftly jump in and fill those spaces with

Most of us have little training in silence.

chatter, whether or not it has any real substance. Everyone feels relieved, although they don't really consider why.

Most of us have little training in silence. We view it as uncomfortable and confusing. So we tend to keep the inner dialogue going just like the outer. Yet, as Pythagorus says, it's in that quiet place where confusion disappears and enlightened thinking comes to us.

As groundbreaking scientists, both Pythagorus and Pascal were studying the nature of the universe. They grappled with the mysteries of numbers, space, time, and other universal truths. Yet the underlying message of each is simple. If you want to understand truths about the universe—or your own personal universe—you must be quiet and learn to be comfortable sitting alone in solitude.

French composer Claude Debussy said, *"Music is the space between the notes."* Without rests there would be only a cacophony of noise. The quiet spaces make the melody of a song. Likewise, learning to be silent involves figuring out a way to enter the spaces between our thoughts and find stillness.

Why is this silence so important? Because that quiet place in our hearts is where we most often sense the Lord's presence—and hear His voice. It is there that we also find His peace.

Most of us need the Lord's help to do this.

Rising Early to Seek Him

Many of the great men and women of faith throughout history spent quiet time with God regularly—usually early in the morning.

David tells us in Psalm 63:1-2 (NKJV):

*O God, You are my God; **Early will I seek You**; My soul thirsts for You; My flesh longs for You in a dry and thirsty land where there is no water. So I have looked for You in the sanctuary, To see Your power and Your glory.*

*O LORD, hear me as I pray; pay attention to my groaning. Listen to my cry for help, my King and my God, for I pray to no one but you. **Listen to my voice in the morning, Lord. Each morning I bring my requests to you and wait expectantly.** (Psalm 5:1-3)*

Daniel had quiet times of prayer daily.

*But when Daniel learned that the law had been signed, he went home and knelt down as usual in his upstairs room, with its windows open toward Jerusalem. **He prayed*** *three times a day, just as he had always done, giving thanks to his God. (Daniel 6:10)*

Job would rise early to pray for his children, and offer sacrifices to purify them.

*When these celebrations ended—sometimes after several days—Job would purify his children. **He would get up early in the morning and offer a burnt offering for each of them.** For Job said to himself, "Perhaps my children have sinned and have cursed God in their hearts." This was Job's regular practice. (Job 1:5)*

Jesus also knew the importance of daily quiet time with the Father. We read in the gospels that He often went out early in the morning to seek silence and pray.

Before daybreak the next morning, *Jesus got up and went out to an isolated place to pray. (Mark 1:35)*

Many notable Christians have adopted similar habits. Robert Murray McCheyne,[3] one of Scotland's most gifted preachers, called the time he spent in communion with God his "noblest and most fruitful employment."

McCheyne said:

I ought to pray before seeing any one. Often when I sleep long, or meet with others early, it is eleven or twelve o'clock before I begin secret prayer. This is a wretched system. It is unscriptural. Christ arose before day and went into a solitary place. David says: "Early will I seek thee;" "Thou shalt early hear my voice." Family prayer loses much of its power and sweetness, and I can do no good to those who come to seek from me. The conscience feels guilty, the soul unfed, the lamp not trimmed. Then when in secret prayer the soul is often out of tune; **I feel it is far better to begin with God—to see his face first, to get my soul near him before it is near another.**[4]

E.M. Bounds,[5] Methodist minister and author of numerous books on prayer, is remembered for his personal devotion to Christ. He prayed every morning from 4-7 a.m. Even during his speaking engagements as an evangelist, he was faithful to keep his early morning time with God.

> *"If God is not first in our thoughts and efforts in the morning, He will be in the last place the remainder of the day."*

In his book *Power Through Prayer*, Bounds writes:

The men who have done the most for God in this world have been early on their knees. He who fritters away the early morning, its opportunity and freshness, in other pursuits than seeking God will make poor headway seeking Him the rest of the day. If God is not first in our thoughts and efforts in the morning, He will be in the last place the remainder of the day.[6]

In the spring of 1841, George Muller experienced new and life-changing understanding of the importance of daily quiet time in the Scriptures and prayer. In his autobiography, he writes:

> *I saw more clearly than ever that the first great and primary business to which I ought to attend every day was to have my soul happy in the Lord. ... How different, when the soul is refreshed and made happy early in the morning, from what it is when, without spiritual preparation, the service, the trials, and the temptations of the day come upon one![7]*

Have you ever made a decision with fresh resolve to get up earlier and spend more time in Bible reading and prayer? I'll admit I have tried to do so at various times in my life and failed miserably. Within a week's time it proved too difficult, and I was back into my old ways. Why? Until I followed Muller's advice I had no long lasting success. In a diary entry from his autobiography, Muller explains:

> *I want to encourage all believers to get into the habit of rising early to meet with God. . . . Someone may ask, "But why should I rise early?" To remain too long in bed is a waste of time. Wasting time is unbecoming a saint who is bought by the precious blood of Jesus. His time and all he has is to be used for the Lord. If we sleep more than is necessary for the refreshment of the body, it is wasting the time the Lord has entrusted us to be used for His glory, for our own benefit, and for the benefit of the saints and unbelievers around us. . . .*

Anyone who spends one, two, or three hours in prayer and meditation before breakfast will soon discover the beneficial effect early rising has on the outward and inward man. . . .

It may be said, "But how shall I set about rising early?" My advice is: Do not delay. Begin tomorrow. But do not depend on your own strength. You may have begun to rise early in the past but have given it up. If you depend on your own strength in this matter, it will come to nothing. In every good work, we must depend on the Lord. If anyone rises so that he may give the time which he takes from sleep to prayer and meditation, let him be sure that satan will try to put obstacles in the way.

Trust in the Lord for help. You will honor Him if you expect help from Him in this matter. Pray for help, expect help, and you will have it. In addition to this, go to bed early. If you stay up late, you cannot rise early. Let no pressure of engagements keep you from going habitually early to bed. If you fail in this, you neither can nor should get up early because your body requires rest.

Rise at once when you are awake. Remain not a minute longer in bed or else you are likely to fall asleep again. Do not be discouraged by feeling drowsy and tired from rising early. This will soon wear off. After a few days you will feel stronger and fresher than when you used to lie an hour or two longer than you needed. Always allow yourself the same hours for sleep. Make no change except on account of sickness.[8]

Why do we try to do anything without the Lord's help? It's the only way to guarantee success!

It could be argued that these great men of faith lived in a different time and weren't as busy as we are. Don't the demands of life today make it impractical for most of us to spend hours in early morning devotions? Yet, I've shared these stories not as a legalistic prescription for when a Christian should pray, but rather as an inspiration to emulate the passion and self-discipline that propelled these men to seek quiet time with the Lord every day. If anything, we need this today more than ever.

Finding Silence, Finding Peace

Is it really more challenging in today's world to find silence? I think most of us would say yes. In the past few decades alone we've adopted more and more of a "constantly busy" culture. Gone are the days when stores and gas stations were closed on Sundays and evenings. At any time of the day or night people are working, eating, shopping, and out of the house.

The world is a noisy place, and it seems to be getting louder all the time. More distractions, faster pace, more things vying for our time. With media, entertainment, and communication constantly at our fingertips and in our pockets,[9] we often have to work hard to do nothing.

Some people grow up in homes where the television is always on. No one is watching. It just occupies space with background noise. Large active families fill the home with activity and the noise level is constant. Some grow up in homes full of arguments and discord, sowing continuous stress and agitation into everyone's lives. These habit patterns carry into our adult lives and often influence how we initially approach God and the time we spend with Him.

Establishing quiet times to commune with the Lord is necessary for anyone who wants a close, intimate relationship with Him. Although morning devotions aren't a command in Scripture, it's clear that many of the great people of faith have testified to it being the optimal time. Early morning devotions (or any other time we choose to devote to being with Him) shouldn't be an obligation or discouraging task. We're to take joy in His communion and find peace in His presence.

It has taken me many years to build silence into my life—to break the habit of always reaching for the radio when I get in the car and to simply enjoy the quietness of His presence as I drive.

> *Establishing quiet times to commune with the Lord is necessary for anyone who wants a close, intimate relationship with Him.*

How refreshed I feel when I spend the time talking with the Lord, instead of always filling my head with mindless noise. I still love music, but I've learned not to let it rule my life.

I've also learned that being a disciple of Christ doesn't mean I have to give up what I enjoy doing. Instead, I seek to balance those activities with keeping Him first in my heart and actions. How much richer and sweeter all of life becomes when I share it with the One who richly gives me all I need for enjoyment![10]

If you're not comfortable with quiet, or if you struggle with racing thoughts, take heart. Jesus Christ is with you, helping, strengthening, and encouraging you in all your endeavors. The lesson of Scripture is that He speaks in a still, small voice.[11] If you are afraid of inner silence, how will you ever be sure of His presence—or know His peace?

Quietness is the classroom where you learn to hear the Lord's voice. Beginners need a quiet place to still their minds, but as you develop this discipline, you learn to carry the stillness with you wherever you go.[12]

Without setting our hearts right with God first thing in the morning, it remains difficult to be still within and hear His voice throughout the day. Start developing regular habits of Scripture reading and prayer. If you are already doing so, seek more. While the rest of the world starts the day with the clock radio blasting the morning news, why not instead wake up to "Great Is Thy Faithfulness" playing? What joy when our first waking thought is one of thanks and praise to Him! Let the Prince of Peace Himself welcome you to the new day, for He is in you . . . just waiting for your call.

If The Heart Wanders

For ten years George Muller had regularly spent time in prayer in the morning, but struggled considerably with his mind wandering. So he changed his habit to meditating on Scripture. As he did, he found he would almost effortlessly go into prayers of thanksgiving, confession, intercession, and supplication. Prayer was no longer such an effort! Reading and meditating on

We simply need less of us and more of Him.

Scripture provided a natural springboard to praise and prayer. He sustained the habit of Bible reading and prayer for the next forty years with much more ease.

The world trains our minds to jump from thought to thought constantly. Television—with its fast moving images— encourages these thought patterns. A wandering mind challenges many Christians during their quiet time with the Lord. Have you ever started praying, only to find a few seconds later you're thinking about what you'll have for dinner that night? When relationship with the Lord becomes a priority, He reveals and helps us with the things we need to change, including learning to control our thoughts.

We *can* learn to focus and quiet our minds as we develop new habit patterns of silence. We simply need less of us and more of Him. Take enough time to tune out life's demands and enter the secret place of His presence. It is only there one can find rest.

> *Those who live in the shelter of the Most High will find rest in the shadow of the Almighty. This I declare about the LORD: He alone is my refuge, my place of safety; he is my God, and I trust him. (Psalm 91:1-2)*

St. Francis de Sales[13] wrote:

> *If the heart wanders or is distracted, bring it back to the point quite gently and replace it tenderly in its Master's presence. And even if you did nothing during the whole of your hour but bring your heart back and place it again in our Lord's presence, though it went away every time you brought it back, your hour will be very well employed. . . . Never be in a hurry; do everything quietly and in a calm spirit.* **Do not lose your inner peace for anything whatsoever, even if your whole world seems upset.**

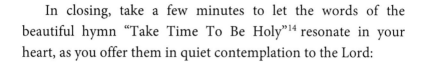

In closing, take a few minutes to let the words of the beautiful hymn "Take Time To Be Holy"[14] resonate in your heart, as you offer them in quiet contemplation to the Lord:

> *Take time to be holy, speak oft with thy Lord;*
> *Abide in Him always, and feed on His Word.*
> *Make friends of God's children, help those who are weak,*
> *Forgetting in nothing His blessing to seek.*
> *Take time to be holy, the world rushes on;*
> *Spend much time in secret, with Jesus alone.*
> *By looking to Jesus, like Him thou shalt be;*
> *Thy friends in thy conduct His likeness shall see.*
> *Take time to be holy, let Him be thy Guide;*
> *And run not before Him, whatever betide.*
> *In joy or in sorrow, still follow the Lord,*
> *And, looking to Jesus, still trust in His Word.*
> *Take time to be holy, be calm in thy soul,*
> *Each thought and each motive beneath His control.*
> *Thus led by His Spirit to fountains of love,*
> *Thou soon shalt be fitted for service above.*

CHAPTER 17

My Sheep Hear My Voice

When our children were small, my husband and I were the coordinators of an active fellowship group that met in our home. Those were the years we were bursting with young families. On a given Sunday, if everyone came, we often had upwards of sixteen children under the age of ten. We began an organized "children's fellowship" to teach them the Scriptures through activities geared toward their age level. One or two of the parents would be responsible for overseeing the kids each week.

Yes, at times it got crazy-noisy. There would be moments of squabbles and crying. We all became used to it. Yet if my son cried out, my ears instantly perked up, even when he was in another room. I clearly recognized his voice over the others— every time!

Mothers have a remarkable way of hearing their child's voice in a group of children playing. Similarly, I've been in a crowded restaurant with friends, stepped out of the room, and could still detect my husband's voice conversing over many others. Often when answering the phone, I recognize the caller's voice within the first two words they speak. Why is this?

Familiarity? Love? Experience?

Perhaps all of the above.

Knowing Mom's Voice

It's long been known that a newborn has an immediate and deep connection with his or her mother and naturally responds to mom's voice. In the womb babies hear sounds at about 30 weeks. Research tells us that babies from all cultures learn to distinguish their mother's voice over others even before birth.

Barbara Kisilevsky, a nursing professor at Queens University in Ontario, did numerous studies with a team of Canadian and Chinese researchers studying infant development. They tested 60 women in the final stage of pregnancy.

All the mothers were tape-recorded as they read a poem out loud. Then the mothers were divided into two groups. Half the fetuses heard the recording of their own mother. The other half heard another mother, but not their own. In both cases, the poem caused a change in the baby's heart rate. The heart rate accelerated among those who heard their own mother's voice, and decelerated among those who heard a voice other than their mother's. Deceleration of the heart rate is "an attention mechanism," Kisilevsky says. The heart-beat among fetuses who heard an unfamiliar voice slowed down, she says, because they were paying close attention to a voice they did not recognize. In other words, they were trying to figure out who was talking. The fact that the heartbeat changed in both cases—up for mom, down for someone else—shows the fetuses "noticed both voices," she says, and could tell one from the other.[1]

Kisilevsky says she suspects the results would have been the same if the mothers had read a phone book or anything else.

They clearly showed that the fetuses recognized voice and speech patterns that distinguish one voice from another, regardless of the content of what was said.

These fascinating studies speak of the innate ability God has placed within every new life to hear, respond to, and know his or her mother. Naturally, as babies come into the world and begin to grow, they learn to also recognize dad's voice and others, and they begin to understand what those voices are saying.

Whose Baby is Crying?

For years, studies have indicated that mothers were better than fathers at identifying their baby's unique cries. Some researchers still insist that a "maternal instinct" rooted at least in part in genetics explains this.

But findings now further suggest that dads are just as adept as moms at recognizing their child from his or her cries. It's simply a matter of learning. In a study, baby cries were recorded, and the mothers and fathers were asked to pick out their child's cries from four other babies. The parents were able to identify their baby's cries 90% of the time on average—if they had regularly spent at least four hours a day with the child. Those who spent less time performed worse at this cry-recognition test. The conclusion was that familiarity and experience, not instinct, hones this ability.[2]

Could the same be true in learning to hear the Lord's voice?

Mary Knew the Master's Voice

After Jesus' horrific death and burial, we learn that Mary, Simon Peter, and another disciple who Jesus loved go to the burial tomb three days later. To their great surprise they find the stone rolled away. The linen wrappings that covered Jesus' body are neatly laid to the side. He is no longer there! The record says the two men then understood the promise that "Jesus must rise from the dead."

Mary enters the tomb, overcome with grief that her Lord is not there. She encounters two angels who say "Dear woman, why are you crying?"

"Because they have taken away my Lord," she replies, "and I don't know where they have put him."

As she turns to leave, someone is standing there—*Jesus*—though she doesn't recognize him. "Dear woman, why are you crying? Who are you looking for?" He says.

Mary thinks it's the gardener.

"Mary!" Jesus says.

Realizing it is Jesus, she cries out *"Rabboni!"* (Hebrew for "teacher.")[3]

What joy must have flooded her heart when she recognized that familiar voice!

Mary had spent much time with her Lord, whom she loved dearly. Although she didn't immediately identify Him in His new resurrected body, as soon as He said her name, she knew it was Him!

God Wanted a Family

As babies respond to their parents, we were created to also respond to our spiritual parent, our Heavenly Father. Since Adam and Eve, God made man and woman with the innate desire and ability to hear His voice. We were designed to enjoy peaceful fellowship with Him.

After humanity's freewill decision to disobey God,[4] the spiritual connection was severed, but a deep longing to know the Creator remains in every heart.[5] One of the many results of getting to know Jesus Christ is that we once again attain perfect communion with our Heavenly Father. With that relationship comes an ability to hear His voice.

As a parent learns to distinguish their child's voice more easily through time spent with him or her, so we can learn to recognize the voice of the Lord as we spend time with Him.

The Lord is Speaking to You

At times, God uses distinct ways to teach us: through circumstances and opportunities, other believers, wise counsel from others, and personal testimonies. He also reveals Himself through nature and His creation, spiritual manifestations and gifts, including healings and miracles, and sometimes through dreams or visions, music, books, and other media.[6]

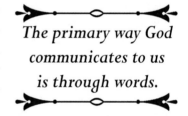

The primary way God communicates to us is through words.

But the primary way God communicates to us is through words—His written Word the Bible—and His speaking to us through the Holy Spirit. His personal speaking will never contradict His written Word. We've talked about the importance of daily Bible reading. Now we'll look more closely at His speaking to us through the Spirit.

God never intended that we go through life on our own, without His guidance and direction. He spoke to Adam in the Garden. God told Noah to build an ark. He spoke to Moses in a burning bush. He verbally promised Abraham a son. On the road to Damascus Paul heard His voice. One of the greatest benefits of salvation in Christ is that of hearing Him speak to us personally through words.

People do not live by bread alone, but by every word (rhema) that comes from the mouth of God. (Matthew 4:4)

While many Christians think "word" in this verse refers to the Bible, it is more than that. It is *rhema* in the Greek,[7] meaning a saying or conversational word. Such words are received through the Holy Spirit. As much as we need food for our daily physical sustenance, we need every word (*rhema*/speaking) that proceeds from the Lord's mouth.

> *As much as we need food for our daily physical sustenance, we need every word that proceeds from the Lord's mouth.*

Long ago God spoke *many times and in many ways to our ancestors through the prophets.* **And now in these final days, he has spoken to us through his Son.** *God promised everything to the Son as an inheritance, and through the Son he created the universe. The Son radiates God's own glory and expresses the very character of God, and he sustains everything by the mighty power of his command. When he had cleansed us from our sins, he sat down in the place of honor at the right hand of the majestic God in heaven. This shows that the Son is far greater than the angels, just as the name God gave him is greater than their names. (Hebrews 1:1-4)*

Long ago, at many times and in many ways, God spoke. In these final days—today—He *has* spoken, and *is* speaking through Jesus Christ. This is not only past tense, but also present. How has God spoken? By revealing His own character and glory in the person and work of Jesus Christ. How is God speaking? By his *rhema* words to us via the Holy Spirit, through Christ within us. Hebrews also tells us the Lord is constantly speaking to us.

> Be careful that you **do not refuse to listen to the One who is speaking.** For if the people of Israel did not escape when they refused to listen to Moses, the earthly messenger, we will certainly not escape if we reject the One who speaks to us from heaven! (Hebrews 12:25)

Radio stations broadcast invisible radio waves that constantly fill the air around us, but only when we turn the radio on and tune in do we hear it. Failure to hear doesn't mean the station isn't transmitting. Similarly, God is continually conveying His voice to us, but few are tuned in. Many Christians struggle to hear His voice, or claim He is silent. In reality, the issue is often with them not turning down the static in their minds and being still enough to listen and hear the broadcast. When He seems silent, it's not because He isn't communicating. It's we who aren't listening.

As discussed in the previous chapter, the noise of life and the distractions of the world often keep us too preoccupied to be quiet and tuned into His speaking. Scripture says it's in stillness that we hear His voice. As God spoke to Elijah in a "still, small voice" or a "gentle whisper," He speaks to us today, as we tune our spiritual ears toward Him.[8] Yet for many, the busyness of daily life drowns out His voice.

Communication with God isn't mouth to ear or mind to mind as in the physical realm. It's spirit to spirit.

For God is Spirit, so those who worship him must worship in spirit and in truth. (John 4:24)

*Anyone who is thirsty may come to me! Anyone who believes in me may come and drink! For the Scriptures declare, "Rivers of living water will flow [rheo-to speak] from his heart." (**When he said "living water," he was speaking of the Spirit,** who would be given to everyone believing in him. But the Spirit had not yet been given, because Jesus had not yet entered into his glory.) (John 7:37b-39)*

The Lord speaks to us in words that come as thoughts. His spirit tells our spirit, and our spirit tells our mind. That's why it can be easy to mistake our own thoughts for His voice. How do we know the difference?

There are no black and white formulas or step-by-step techniques to teach us how to identify God's voice. But I believe as the parent learns to more easily recognize the cries of the child through spending time with the child, so we learn to discern and hear the Lord's voice as we spend time with Him. And the Holy Spirit, our guide to all truth—plus its conformity to Scripture—helps us make the connection. All we need do is ask.

⎯⎯⎯⎯⎯⎯⎯ ◄᳁᳁᳁᳁᳁► ⎯⎯⎯⎯⎯⎯⎯

Hearing Our Shepherd—It's All About Relationship

In John 10 Jesus makes some profound statements about His relationship with us. Clearly, He wants us to hear His voice.

> . . . anyone who sneaks over the wall of a sheepfold, rather than going through the gate, must surely be a thief and a robber! But the one who enters through the gate is the shepherd of the sheep. The gatekeeper opens the gate for him, and **the sheep recognize his voice and come to him**. He calls his own sheep by name and leads them out. After he has gathered his own flock, he walks ahead of them, and **they follow him because they know his voice**. They won't follow a stranger; they will run from him because they don't know his voice. (John 10:1-5)

Jesus speaks about Himself as the Shepherd and us as the sheep. In verse 3 He says the sheep recognize or hear His voice. He doesn't say the sheep might hear His voice, or should hear His voice, or can hear His voice. He emphatically declares that the sheep DO hear His voice!

> Look! I stand at the door and knock. **If you hear my voice** and open the door, I will come in, and we will share a meal together as friends. Those who are victorious will sit with me on my throne, just as I was victorious and sat with my Father on his throne. (Revelation 3:20-21)

It's all about relationship. And key to relationship is hearing the voice of the one to whom we are relating.

To fathom the great beauty of the connection we have with Jesus as our Shepherd, let's look at it in more detail. It helps to understand the role of shepherds in ancient Palestine. In those days, sheep were a valuable source of wool for clothing and food.

Since the sheep recognized the shepherd's unique voice, they would go to him, and he would lead them out.

The shepherd's life was to care for and protect the sheep; to give them all they needed. He would lead them to pasture and water, keep them together, calm them, tend to their wounds, and rescue them from briar patches and wolves.

Sheep are dumb, near-sighted, skittish creatures. If left on their own, they can destroy a pasture. They are prone to wandering off and will repeatedly roam into dangerous situations, not learning to avoid them.

The shepherd would give each sheep and lamb in the flock its own name, and the sheep actually came to respond to their names. At times, the flocks of different shepherds would intermingle while grazing. To separate them, a shepherd would go out and call together his sheep. Since the sheep recognized the shepherd's unique voice, they would go to him, and he would lead them out.

The shepherd never drove the sheep from behind, but instead led them by walking ahead or alongside the sheep, and they followed him. Verses 3 and 4 of John 10 tell us Jesus also calls us by name and leads us. He goes before us, and we follow, for we know His voice.

The tools the shepherd used were simple. He always carried his staff—a long stick with a curved hook at the end. If one of the sheep started to stray, the shepherd would reach out with his staff and gently pull it back. He also carried a rod in his belt—a club about three feet long, which was used to drive off wild animals or defend the flock against robbers who might try to steal a sheep. The shepherd often had to lead the sheep through dark, narrow valleys where animals or thieves were hiding. He would walk ahead of them to make sure the way was safe, before leading the sheep safely through.

Isaiah 40:11, speaking of the coming Messiah, says:

He will feed his flock like a shepherd. He will carry the lambs in his arms, holding them close to his heart. He will gently lead the mother sheep with their young.

The shepherd had to know where to lead the sheep to find enough food and water to survive. In many regions, pastures and wells were scarce. If he couldn't find enough grass, it wasn't unusual for the shepherd to spend his whole day cutting the branches of trees, so the sheep could feed on the green leaves and tender twigs.

Often the shepherd would be seen carrying young lambs that weren't strong enough yet to walk any distance. The verse in Isaiah again shows that Jesus will likewise gently lead and care for His flock, to get them all safely to their destination.

Every evening, the shepherd led the sheep into a fold—a corral made from stones and bushes piled together to form a large circle. Each sheep had to enter the fold through a narrow entrance. The shepherd held out his rod for each to pass under, and as it did he would quickly examine it to make sure none were injured. Ezekiel referred to this when he prophesied *"I will make you pass under the rod, and I will bring you into the bond of the covenant."* [9]

Once the flock was safely inside the fold, the shepherd would lay down along the entrance, so no sheep could wander out and no predators could get in. He literally became a protecting door to keep the sheep safe. Again, this closely parallels Jesus protecting us, as seen in the next verses of John 10:

I tell you the truth, I am the gate for the sheep. All who came before me were thieves and robbers. But the true sheep did not listen to them. Yes, I am the gate. Those who come in through me will be saved. They will come and go freely and will find good pastures. The thief's purpose is to steal and kill and destroy. My purpose is to give them a rich and satisfying life. I am the good shepherd. The good shepherd sacrifices his life for the sheep. (John 10:7b-11)

In ancient Israel, a shepherd often owned the flock he oversaw. Some shepherds were hired to tend to the flock, and instead of being paid money were given a share of the produce from the flock. There were other shepherds who were paid a set amount of money; a daily wage. They were the hired hands. These shepherds never came to know the sheep, nor did the sheep know them. They were only in business for the money. When danger came, a hired hand would sometimes flee for safety, leaving the flock defenseless.

A hired hand will run when he sees a wolf coming. He will abandon the sheep because they don't belong to him and he isn't their shepherd. And so the wolf attacks them and scatters the flock. The hired hand runs away because he's working only for the money and doesn't really care about the sheep. (John 10:12-13)

Palestine was filled with desolate hills and valleys, and high cliffs that plunged into deep ravines. The watchful shepherd protected the sheep and safely guided them along the way. After spending years caring for his flock, the shepherd was ready to risk his life for his beloved sheep.

Some sheep were gentle and obedient and stayed close by the shepherd. Others would carelessly stray away or linger behind the flock. If a sheep wandered away, the shepherd would search for it until he found it, at times risking his own well-being to bring it safely back to the fold.

I am the good shepherd; I know my own sheep, and they know me, just as my Father knows me and I know the Father. *So I sacrifice my life for the sheep. I have other sheep, too, that are not in this sheepfold. I must bring them also.* **They will listen to my voice, and there will be one flock with one shepherd.** *(John 10:14-16)*

The beautiful imagery of the shepherd and his sheep in John 10 signifies the great love that Christ has for each one of us. He calls us by name, cares for us, protects us, leads us, and guides us along our way. He tends to our wounds and gently pulls us back into the fold when we wander off.

But the main point is this: only when the sheep learned to hear the voice of their shepherd were they able to obey and receive protection and sustenance.

In the Old Testament, David was a shepherd before he became king. In Psalm 23, he called God his shepherd. This familiar passage takes on deeper meaning when we understand the significance of the shepherd/sheep relationship. As you read, allow it to speak comfort to your heart.

The LORD is my shepherd; I have all that I need. He lets me rest in green meadows; he leads me beside peaceful streams. He renews my strength. He guides me along right paths, bringing honor to his name. Even when I walk through the darkest valley, I will not be afraid, for you are close beside me. Your rod and your staff protect and comfort me. You prepare a feast for me in the presence of my enemies. You honor me by anointing my head with oil. My cup overflows with blessings. Surely your goodness and unfailing love will pursue me all the days of my life, and I will live in the house of the LORD forever.

> *As God was David's shepherd in the Old Testament, He is ours today through Jesus Christ.*

As God was David's shepherd in the Old Testament, He is ours today through Jesus Christ. As we choose to spend time with the Shepherd and learn the sound of His voice, we gain all the benefits that a good shepherd has to offer!

Drawing Near to the Shepherd

Do you love the Lord Jesus Christ? Do you yearn to rest in His presence and hear His voice?

Share conversation with the Master throughout the day, as you would with a good friend, remembering that He is there—readily willing to speak and share all you need to be victorious in life. Only through spending time in His presence and care do we come to know Him, and learn to recognize His voice. Remember *"come to me . . . and I will give you rest"?*[10] We must each allow His peace to direct our hearts.

> And **let the peace that comes from Christ rule in your hearts**. *(Colossians 3:15a)*

As we experience life—with all its twists and turns—in partnership with Christ our Shepherd, we grow in learning to hear and obey His voice. We must draw near to the Shepherd and walk in His care. Day by day He leads us into a more powerful walk of faith. I believe we can all learn to hear His voice with clarity, consistency, and confidence. It's part of His plan for blessing our lives!

CHAPTER 18

Your Best State of Mind

After 35 years in the same house, it was time for a change. My parents were ready to leave the bustling New York City suburbs and enjoy retirement in the "country." So my Dad ambitiously built a second house about 70 miles north in Dutchess County. With 54 acres of property, it sat high on a hill with spectacular views of the Taconic Mountains in Connecticut.

Visiting them meant an overnight stay for my family. When the boys were small they loved seeing deer, turkeys, and other wildlife right in their grandparents' backyard. In this vast, open playground they could explore and roam freely. For the first time my parents had a pool, which became the centerpiece for many family barbeques and gatherings in the summertime.

I'll always remember one particular visit. It was during the year I described in the opening of chapter one, when I had endured months on end of stomach ailments, with little to no relief. The latest medication I tried—yet another acid reducer—again did nothing. Despite my repeated prayers for healing, I had unintentionally fallen into the vicious cycle of worrying about my symptoms, which of course only made them worse. The acid reflux and ache in my stomach became so constant I found it hard to eat. As the mother of two children under six, I couldn't afford to be like this and do what I needed to do. My condition became all-consuming as I struggled to make it through each day. In short, I was a wreck.

Would things ever be right again?

As I sat at the kitchen table after dinner talking to my mother, everyone else was in the living room watching "Jeopardy," part of my Dad's nightly routine. Suddenly we heard the boys' voices rise in cries of frustration. They were at it again—no doubt both grabbing at a toy.

"I get so tired of hearing them fighting. Sometimes I wish they would just go away for awhile!" I blurted out to my mother.

"Oh, they're just being normal," she said. "They go through these stages. In time it will change."

I went on, complaining to her about the boys and other things, how difficult life had recently been, and how hard it was to take care of the kids while feeling so miserable myself.

"But you have so much to be thankful for," she said. *"Why don't you focus on those things for awhile?"*

Bam! With those words a big light bulb went on in my head. Where had my thoughts been lately? Dwelling on the negative and complaining, or on the positive and being grateful?

"Children grow. They won't be like this forever," my mother continued. "Your boys are healthy, smart, and blessed to have you home with them. That's a lot to be thankful for. Just enjoy them. Things will get better," she again reassured me.

The next morning I went to the Scriptures and looked up verses about giving thanks. A passage in 1 Thessalonians especially caught my attention:

Always be joyful. Never stop praying. **Be thankful in all circumstances,** *for this is God's will for you who belong to*

Christ Jesus. (1 Thessalonians 5:16-18)

Could God really be saying to give thanks for all circumstances—irrespective of my situation? How could I give thanks for feeling sick? I then noticed it didn't say, "give thanks *for* all circumstances," but "*in*" all circumstances. The Holy Spirit clearly had convicted my heart through my mother's words, reminding me of God's will that I give thanks. Yet it still seemed difficult to give thanks for what I considered a negative situation— especially one I had immersed my mind in for so many days.

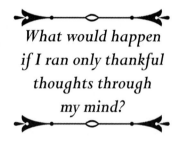

What would happen if I ran only thankful thoughts through my mind?

I've long held the belief that if we could always think the whole and pure thoughts of God, our bodies would be healthy. So much illness is self-inflicted by our unbelief. After all, God designed our minds to hold His Word, and our bodies to heal themselves. He desires us to have perfect health. Yet at that time in my life I had unknowingly allowed myself to slip deeper and deeper into the negative mental ruts of complaining, bitterness, and self-pity. As I realized this, I wondered, "Was this powerful enough to be making me sick?"

What would happen if I ran only thankful thoughts through my mind, and refused to entertain the negative and complaining ones? I decided to try it out. As I prayed, I humbly asked the Lord for forgiveness for the destructive mindset I had developed, and to help release me from it so that once again I could do His will. I asked Him to remind me of the many things I have to be thankful for, and to help me be grateful.

A New Thankful Beginning

Starting that day, I intentionally tried to think thankful thoughts. Every time I found myself slipping into a negative thought, I immediately replaced it with something to be grateful for. With new resolve in my heart we headed home. I was determined to develop new thankful thought patterns. With His help I was going to do it!

It was easy to start with the big things. I'm thankful for my home, which gives me shelter and warmth. I'm thankful for my family whom I love and who loves me. I'm thankful for clothes to wear and food to eat. As I moved through the days I became thankful for the things I handled and used—my car, the refrigerator, my cappuccino maker!

I moved to a deeper level as I became thankful for eyes to see my children in front of me, the lush green grass, and a beautiful sunset. For ears to hear the music I enjoy and my husband say "goodnight." As I prepared salads I was thankful for fresh vegetables to enjoy and be nourished by. But where did those vegetables come from? I thanked God for the farmers who grew them, the trucks that transported them, the grocery store that sold them.

I could not change my circumstances, but I could change how I perceived them.

I started to praise God for His amazing creation and His goodness in blessing me so richly. I thanked Him for Jesus Christ, alive within me, and for the ability to hear His voice. I thanked Him for the freedom I enjoy, and the peace He provides.

Over the following days I began to gradually feel the heaviness that had encased my heart for so long lighten. I could not change my circumstances, but I could change how I perceived them. I continued to trust God for release from my stomach woes, and though they were still there, I began to feel hopeful.

The Lord showed me that when my boys' voices rose, my stomach would tighten. This had been happening multiple times a day. Day after day. Week after week. A conditioned response rooted in negative thoughts. It was time to cut the root!

The Open Door to Healing

Thankfulness restored my joy in the Lord. It reminded me of His presence. When I found His presence, my heart found rest. I realized He had never left me and wanted to help me overcome. He wanted me healed. Thought by thought I focused on praising Him for His goodness to me, and thanking Him for everything around me—even in the midst of my adversity.

Within a few weeks my stomach disorders lessened, and in six weeks time they were completely gone! No amount of doctor visits, tests, or drugs had helped. God alone delivered me and restored my body to health. Thanks and praise to Him opened the door to release me from my own self-inflicted mental and physical illness, and allow me to receive His healing goodness.

As praise and gratitude put me in proper relationship with God, I found His peace again—which had never left me, but which I hadn't sensed for a long time. With my heart at peace I could hear His voice as He revealed to me the things I needed to know. And with His help I changed the things I needed to change. How good it felt to laugh again! All these things worked together to allow my body to naturally heal and restore itself to the health that God intended.

I continue to praise Him for His goodness to me!

An Attitude of Gratitude—Your Best State of Mind

Countless studies reveal scientific evidence of life-changes through positive, thankful thoughts in our minds. Gratitude affects our total being—mentally, physically, and spiritually. It makes us happier, healthier, and strengthens our emotions; develops our personality, boosts our career, gives us resilience to life's adversities, and in general, just makes us feel good!

Much is written about the benefits of gratitude and how it increases happiness on many levels. Socially, thankful people have more friendships, deeper relationships, and healthier marriages. Gratitude causes people to be more optimistic, less self-centered and materialistic, and it increases self-esteem. Those who are thankful store fewer resentments and less bitterness. Being thankful increases productivity in work, improves decision-making, and helps achieve goals. Healthwise, thankfulness has been shown to produce greater longevity, more relaxation, increased energy, better sleep, and less sickness.[1]

Thankfulness is a lost art in today's culture.

Small annoyances don't seem so important when I'm thankful. I feel energized. More alive. More confident about myself and the world around me.

Many of us grew up without any examples or training in gratitude. Simple acts like a prayer of thanks before a meal speak loudly. Thankfulness is a lost art in today's culture. Especially in places like America, where most people's physical needs are met. They spend much of their lives focusing more on what they don't have than on what they do have. In a secular article on giving thanks, author Bob Burg says:

For whatever reason it is, for the first 35 years of my life I tended to focus more on what I didn't have than on what I had. Thus, it didn't matter how much I had; since I didn't truly appreciate it, it was as if it didn't exist. What did exist? That which I didn't have or didn't like. And, my level of happiness reflected this.[2]

Thankfulness Leads to Praise

Thankfulness and praise are inextricably linked together. They put us in right relationship with God. We're to enter His gates with thanksgiving and His courts with praise.[3] As we do, peace, comfort, and joy can fill our hearts. For the person with the Spirit of God residing within, thankfulness not only reaps the many benefits discussed, but also opens the windows of heaven, allowing spiritual blessings to flow freely. The sacrifice of praise and thanksgiving centers my being on Him, allowing me to release my burdens into His care, and view life more from His perspective. Remember Philippians 4:6-7? Giving thanks is mentioned here:

*Don't worry about anything; instead, pray about everything. Tell God what you need, and **thank him for all he has done. Then you will experience God's peace**, which exceeds anything we can understand. His peace will guard your hearts and minds as you live in Christ Jesus.*

Thankfulness is not a formula. It's the language of love to our Heavenly Father, the giver of all good gifts. It opens the doors of communication to the God who created us to glorify Him. By giving thanks frequently, we learn to pray always (1

Thessalonians 5:16-18). Thankfulness lays a solid foundation on which to approach God and communicate with Him. When our minds are focused on thanking Him in all circumstances, there is no room for worrying or complaining. Negative thought patterns weaken and fall away through habits of praise.

In Luke 6, Jesus tells us we're to leap for joy—even when we're hungry, when we weep, when people hate us, exclude us, and speak evil of us for following Christ . . . *"When that happens, be happy! Yes, leap for joy."* [4]

In 2 Corinthians 12:9-10 Paul says:

Each time he [the Lord] said, "My grace is all you need. My power works best in weakness." So now I am glad to boast about my weaknesses, so that the power of Christ can work through me. That's why I take pleasure in my weaknesses, and in the insults, hardships, persecutions, and troubles that I suffer for Christ. For when I am weak, then I am strong.

The Psalms continually speak of joy in the midst of troubles, in the context of thanks and praise. Read Psalm 30, where David concludes *"You have turned my mourning into joyful dancing."* But how do we leap for joy under distressing circumstances? How do we give thanks in all things then?

We must choose to walk the high road of thankfulness.

Blessings and sorrows intermingle freely in the fallen world in which we live. A focus on problems and adversity defeats many Christians. They walk through the day with a dark cloud overhead, overshadowing their thoughts with negativity. Their hearts find no rest in the Lord. They take the low road.

Thankfulness takes the sting out of adversity. It doesn't remove present problems but instead draws my focus onto Christ, the Overcomer who gives me strength. Suddenly I'm more resilient in the face of setbacks. Small frustrations don't seem so significant anymore. Rather than trying to control my own destiny, gratitude—even for my present difficulties—helps me yield myself to Him who gives me peace, even in the midst of trials.

We must choose to walk the high road of thankfulness.

———————◄◖═◗►———————

The Old Testament book of Exodus gives account of the people of Israel after they left Egypt and were traveling to the Promised Land. Along the way they began to bicker and complain. We read:

> *There, too, the whole community of Israel complained about Moses and Aaron. "If only the LORD had killed us back in Egypt," they moaned. "There we sat around pots filled with meat and ate all the bread we wanted. But now you have brought us into this wilderness to starve us all to death." (Exodus 16:2-3)*

But God took care of His people. In the next verse He says "I'm going to rain down food from heaven for you." From that time on, every morning the ground was covered with food (manna). The people then complained about only having manna to eat. In Numbers we hear them complain, "Give us meat to eat!"[5] So God sent them quail. The record says they ate so much quail they got sick from it. Then they complained that they would die of thirst. In Exodus they also complained of thirst, and God caused water to gush out of the rocks so they could drink.[6] The Israelites were good at complaining. God delivered them from slavery and gave them manna to eat; yet still they were not grateful.

Scripture says their complaining hearts displeased God.[7] Even when God responded to their grumbles and helped them, they still didn't stop and express any gratitude to Him. Our complaining also displeases God, because it shows little thanks for what He has done in the past, and little faith for what He can do now. We say we trust God. But do we really believe He has a hand on every detail of our lives? Jesus reminds us that the Father knows how many hairs are on our heads.[8] So why do we struggle to believe that He is more intimately concerned with our lives than we are? God is directing everything and working out all that happens for our good.

And we know that God causes everything to work together for the good of those who love God and are called according to his purpose for them. (Romans 8:28)

Gratitude grows our trust in God and gives us joy in the midst of difficulties. This is a great paradox—to give thanks for adversity—and by doing so find joy. In his quest for finding joy in the Lord, Merlin Carothers put this to the test. His results were astounding.

How to Find Joy in Every Season of Life
As a young man, Merlin Carothers was far from God's heart. While serving in the Army during World War II he

continuously challenged the system and got in trouble. But his life changed dramatically when he found Christ. During the Korean War he volunteered for the chaplaincy and found himself counseling other servicemen in the ways of God.

Years later, he again served as an Army chaplain during the Vietnam War. It was during this time that he realized he had little joy in his life. He began to ask the Lord to teach him how to cultivate a joyful heart. He learned about being thankful. He sought to understand the command to *"always be joyful"* in 1 Thessalonians 4:16, and how to give thanks not for all things, but *in* all things.

Merlin found that as he focused on thanking God at all times, his trust in Him grew. He became joyful more often, even through difficult times. In the book *Prison to Praise*, Carothers shares his journey from a life of emptiness and sorrow to one of great joy in Christ. He concludes that if we truly serve a sovereign God, He has authority and is in control of our lives. God allows us to go through challenges to draw closer to Him. In the end, the promise that everything works together for the good of those who love God and are called according to His purpose for them rings true.

Carothers writes:

I have come to believe that the prayer of praise is the highest form of communion with God, and one that always releases a great deal of power into our lives. Praising Him is not something we do because we feel good; rather it is an act of obedience. Often the prayer of praise is done in sheer teeth-gritting willpower; yet when we persist in it, somehow the power of God is released into us and into the situation. At first in a trickle perhaps, but later in a growing stream that finally floods us and washes away the old hurts and scars.[9]

In his book, Carothers shares many stories of the people to whom he taught these truths. These inspiring testimonies of God's deliverance and joy are confirmation of the blessings of gratitude.

Entering His Presence and Finding Peace

Peace comes from faith in Christ, and the ability to trust Him over my circumstances. Enter His gates with thanksgiving and His courts with praise. Offer Him the sacrifices of thanks and declare His works with rejoicing.

Thank Him for the amazing gift of the Holy Spirit, by which you can hear the Lord speaking. Give thanks to the One worthy of all our thanks and praise. Praise Him that His ways are not yours. Lay at His feet your anxious thoughts and feel the embrace of His strong arms. As you thank Him for all things in your life, allow the joy of His presence to fill you. The joy of the Lord *is* your strength.[10]

Instead of only seeking Him, you soon discover you are found by Him. In the quietness of His presence your innermost being floods with His peace. You share it with Him in wordless silence. You bask in the warmth of His love. As you continue to dwell with the Lord, the ears of your heart open to receive from Him—a reminder that you are never alone. You gain a new perspective on life—His perspective. And He responds to the longing of your heart to be like Him.

CHAPTER 19

Peacemakers in a Troubled World

Charles Carl Roberts IV, an American milk truck driver, drove to a small one-room Amish schoolhouse in Nickel Mines, Pennsylvania, on a crisp, fall morning in October 2006. Full of evil intent and heavily armed, he stormed into the school, barricaded the doors and held students hostage, ordering them to line up against the chalkboard. By the time the ordeal ended, he senselessly gunned down five young schoolgirls and wounded five others before taking his own life. The entire pacifist Amish community lay in shock.

But in a stunning act *the night of the shootings*, elders from the Amish community went to the widow of the gunman and extended forgiveness and grace to her and her children. Mrs. Roberts was a murderer's wife, but also a victim and a grieving widow. The Amish refused to let one man's violence and aggression breed unrest within their community.[1]

Violence such as this confounds us. We fear it, yet embrace it. While it horrifies us, it also entertains us. How many people would be the first to say they hate the violence in our world? Yet many of these same people regularly entertain themselves with violent images on television, or spend countless hours playing video games that turn violence into fun.

The viciousness in our culture has never been higher. Experiences of road rage and aggression in sports abound. Talk of peace is no longer vogue. Just a few decades ago peace symbols were worn around our necks, and seen on bumper stickers and book covers. Not so much today. If provoked, too many are quick to fight. Surely everyone knows that peacemaking is too idealistic in today's world, don't they?

Everyone except Jesus.

Blessed are the peacemakers, for they shall be called sons of God. (Matthew 5:9)

Jesus calls all His followers to pursue and display peace as a way of life.

Peacemaking is Risky Business

Peace on earth sounds great, doesn't it? It also sounds like a trite phrase on a Christmas card, a poster from the 1970s, or a promise made by a politician to win a few extra votes in the next election.

Peace on earth is more than political and economic stability or the absence of unrest or war between nations. Peacemaking requires more than bringing peace between two conflicting parties. True peacemakers actively work at conveying peace in all of life's relationships. They are often the ones to bring wholeness and well-being to the world's alienated, downtrodden, and forgotten.

To study some of the world's great peacemakers of our time, read the biographies of people such as Mother Teresa, Martin Luther King Jr., Eleanor Roosevelt, Nelson Mandela, and

Mahatma Gandhi. Each of these people, in their own ways, fought for change in the world and peace among people.

Being such a peacemaker may be an honorable pursuit, but it's also dangerous. These peacemakers must actively engage in the world around them. Many end up as victims themselves. Mahatma Gandhi, whose work in India and South Africa inspired movements for civil rights and freedom across the world, survived at least five assassination attempts before being shot and killed on January 30, 1948.

In October 1964, Martin Luther King, Jr. received the Nobel Peace Prize for his work in combating racial inequality through nonviolent civil disobedience. Six months later he was killed by a sniper's bullet while standing on a motel balcony in Memphis, Tennessee.

Countless others have sacrificed their lives or been imprisoned while standing up for their ideals. Peacemakers such as these don't consider the possibility of their death as grounds to quietly acquiesce to evil.

Called To Be Peacemakers

The work of peacemakers is distinctly different from *peacekeepers*. Peacekeepers work hard to maintain the status quo. They confront no one and challenge nothing the world says is okay. They try to keep a lid on conflict of any way, shape, or form. In contrast, a godly peace*maker* calls sin what it is and leads others to repentance and change. A peacemaker actively challenges injustice and confronts evil.

The term "peacemaking" is often associated with a strongly pacifistic anti-military stance, or a liberal political agenda. Irrespective of our views on these things, it's important that we detach ourselves from worldly definitions and search out the biblical significance of what it means to be a peacemaker. We need to remember that Jesus is the one who blesses the peacemakers and shows us how they live.

Jesus came without violence into an evil world. He fought not with weapons but with words. Peacemakers understand the futility of violence. To be a true peacemaker, one cannot participate in the violence of the culture. Blessed are the peacemakers, because their lives show Christ's love to an evil and dying world. They reflect the ministry of Christ Himself. Godly peacemaking requires extraordinary conviction and strength of character. Such a peacemaker presents Christlike ideals to a world that often says otherwise. Therefore, true godly peacemakers remain rare in our culture.

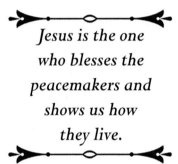

Jesus is the one who blesses the peacemakers and shows us how they live.

As Christians, we all share the mission to bring peace to the world. We're wrong if we think peacemaking requires a major offense or public campaign. Every time we see need or hurt in those around us, do we look to serve them or avoid them? These are our greatest opportunities for peacemaking. They occur daily, most often in the routines of life.

As we respond with love toward annoying co-workers, rude neighbors, or the street beggar, our lives display the peace of Christ to the world—and we often inspire others to act similarly. In exploring our role as godly peacemakers, it may help to break it down into three major areas of our lives—the church, the home, and the world around us.

Living As Peacemakers in the Church

When the peace of God rules in our hearts, it should extend outward and touch all the important relationships in our lives— our family, friends, and the church. Let's look first at some of necessary ingredients to be peacemakers in the church.

*Therefore **let us pursue the things which make for peace** and the things by which one may edify another. (Romans 14:19 NKJV)*

***Work at living in peace with everyone**, and work at living a holy life, for those who are not holy will not see the Lord. (Hebrews 12:14)*

*Make every effort to keep yourselves united in the Spirit, **binding yourselves together with peace**. (Ephesians 4:3)*

The verbs in these verses, "pursue," "work at," "make every effort," "binding," clearly demonstrate that peacemaking is not passive but requires intentional action on our part. In the church we are to edify one another, endeavor to live holy lives, and seek peace with each other. As we do so, it binds us together as one body. How is this accomplished? Ephesians 4:2 tells us:

Always be humble and gentle. Be patient with each other, making allowance for each other's faults because of your love.

Let's face it. When we cohabit with people long enough, it's inevitable that problems arise. At some point something about me is bound to offend or annoy you, and likewise you with me.

If we allow offenses to take root in our hearts, our relationship fractures and seeds of division are sown. This is exactly what the devil wants to see happen in the church!

Division also takes root through the selfishness of people when they seek their own good rather than the benefit of the church community as a whole.

> *Don't be selfish; don't try to impress others. Be humble, thinking of others as better than yourselves. (Philippians 2:3)*

The subtlety of pride all too easily slips in when we fail to view others as God does. We are to seek peace among our brothers and sisters because we are one body in Christ, united by His spirit.

If we have a complaint or criticism, we need to communicate it with humility—realizing we *could* be wrong—and not allow it to fester. We must seek to look at one another as God does, realizing that our brother or sister is precious in His sight. Therefore, I need to treat each person with gentleness and love.

We also make peace by being patient with each other. The call for patience in Ephesians 4:2 implies that some will frustrate us at times. They won't serve as much as we think they should. They'll be too slow at responding or getting things done. They won't change quickly enough. Some in the church pray too long or too short. Some talk too much. We must all learn to put up with each other's faults and weaknesses, exercise patience, and pursue peace with one another. It's simply part of walking in love. And it's the love of God that covers the multitude of sins.

Most important of all, continue to show deep love for each other, for love covers a multitude of sins. (1 Peter 4:8)

It is certainly right to confront a brother or sister who sins, but loving patience is necessary for all the other bothersome little things that irritate us.

Church unity can never be taken for granted. It doesn't just happen. It requires constant diligence. If you see the beginnings of division, nip it in the bud before it blossoms into conflict. If a brother or sister offends you, go to him or her and seek resolution. When two people are stuck in disagreement, try to help them understand each other. If something in the church gets on your nerves, don't start complaining to others before going to leadership. This kind of "canvassing" can quickly become one of the most destructive forces of division. Rather, when there is a disagreement, go to those responsible and talk directly, honestly, and humbly. When we do this, relationships are often strengthened—and everyone goes home with a peaceful heart.[2]

Peacemaking in the church requires forgiveness.

Peacemaking in the church requires forgiveness. Colossians 3:13-15 makes this clear:

Make allowance for each other's faults, and forgive anyone who offends you. Remember, the Lord forgave you, so you must forgive others. Above all, clothe yourselves with love, which binds us all together in perfect harmony. And let the peace that comes from Christ rule in your hearts. For as members of one body you are called to live in peace. And always be thankful.

Forgiveness is not optional behavior for the Christian. When we hold on to offenses, when we say we forgive but don't actually do so, if we formulate plans to get even, or avoid having anything to do with the person who offended us—we are undermining the unity of the Spirit that binds us together in the body of Christ. This kind of behavior often contributes more to the demise of the church than the one who wronged us.

Instead of always seeking justice when someone wrongs us, simple forgiveness is often the most loving action to take. Let God take care of others' "dirty laundry" (a/k/a transgressions). When we forgive, relationships are reinforced and renewed, and most of all, our own hearts are freed so they can remain at peace.

Living As Peacemakers in the Home

Everything necessary for peacemaking in the church also applies to the home. Humility, patience, forgiveness, and love begin at home. Yet why is it often the hardest to live out these virtues with those who mean the most to us?

After being out in the world all day exercising patience, forgiveness, and love with those at work or school, it's easy to go home and be none of those things to the people I live with. My spouse and children often get the worst of me—the impatience, the unforgiveness, and insensitivity that so often slips out of me. It seems to be human nature that we "let our hair down" with those closest to us. Somehow thankfulness for what is familiar easily gets forgotten.

But because I am so human, I need to work doubly hard to live out my faith with my family, first and foremost, not last and least. Even Christian families often substitute good deeds for true peacemaking in the home. Without honesty, forgiveness, and love, they subtly begin to store bitterness against one another. Walls of hostility gradually go up around their hearts. Forgiveness is not pretending everything is okay and doing nothing. Instead, forgiveness runs to fix small offenses before they escalate into major issues. Only genuine forgiveness brings the wholeness and peace that God desires to family relationships.

Often forgiveness is lacking simply because the one who wounded us is unwilling to admit the wrong and ask for forgiveness. Isn't it much easier to forgive someone when they come to us and say, "I'm so sorry. I was wrong. Please forgive me." Of course it is!

Parents often find it difficult to admit to their children when they make a mistake, especially if they've been working hard to set a good example. The thought of humbling oneself to a child can be uncomfortable and humiliating. But when we swallow our pride and apologize, admitting our mistake and asking for forgiveness, it grows roots of peacemaking that run deep. How else can I expect my child to admit his or her mistakes and learn to forgive if they don't see me modeling it? Such a simple exchange, when made from the heart, usually ends with a hug and everyone feels better. Life can go on. Peace is restored.

Another common situation arises when both parties are at fault for something. Perhaps you feel you were just a little bit wrong, and the other person was mostly to blame. Love refuses to wait for the greater offender to initiate "I'm sorry." If you have contributed to an offense to any degree, why not seek and extend forgiveness quickly?

If you've been involved in Christian service for some time, perhaps you've seen forgiveness in operation within families— even in the "big" things. The wife who forgives her husband for being unfaithful in their marriage. A daughter who forgives her father for not being involved in her life as a child. The son who forgives a parent for years of alcohol abuse. These are powerful examples of peacemaking in action.

Peacemaking begins in our closest relationships—in our homes and marriages, our families and friendships. If it's happening there and in the church, it becomes easier to live as peacemakers in the world.

Living As Peacemakers in the World

To bring God's peace to the world, begin by looking right in front of you. You'll find opportunities to be a peacemaker in your neighborhood, your office, your school, and your local supermarket. Ask the Lord to show you how you can share His peace with those you interact with each day. Here are a few things to keep in mind while doing so:

Share Christ's Work on the Cross

Many mainstream peacemaking efforts today, even among churches, seek to make peace among people without mentioning the one who is our source for peace, Jesus Christ. In an effort to find healing and reconciliation through support groups and therapy techniques, Christ is often minimized into a vague "higher power" or neglected entirely. How can we expect to bring peace to the world without talking about the finished work of Jesus Christ on the cross? Only the good news of Christ invites people to renounce their sin and be reconciled to God—

so they too experience His perfect peace and live as peacemakers.

Be an Example of Christ

We must live with the attitudes of Christ as reflected in Philippians 2:1-11:

Is there any encouragement from belonging to Christ? Any comfort from his love? Any fellowship together in the Spirit? Are your hearts tender and compassionate? Then make me truly happy by agreeing wholeheartedly with each other, loving one another, and working together with one mind and purpose.

Don't be selfish; don't try to impress others. Be humble, thinking of others as better than yourselves. Don't look out only for your own interests, but take an interest in others, too. You must have the same attitude that Christ Jesus had.

To put others ahead of ourselves is a paradigm of peacemaking that speaks loudly to a self-centered world.

Though he was God, he did not think of equality with God as something to cling to. Instead, he gave up his divine privileges; he took the humble position of a slave and was born as a human being. When he appeared in human form, he humbled himself in obedience to God and died a criminal's death on a cross.

Therefore, God elevated him to the place of highest honor and gave him the name above all other names, that at the name of Jesus every knee should bow, in heaven and on earth and under the earth, and every tongue confess that Jesus Christ is Lord, to the glory of God the Father.

Christ's model of self-sacrifice shows us how to live. To put others ahead of ourselves is a paradigm of peacemaking that speaks loudly to a self-centered world.

Live at Peace With Others
Do all that you can to live in peace with everyone. (Romans 12:18)

For the Christian, peace should flow out of us when we're living in His presence. It need not be a difficult task to strive or work for, but a natural outcome of being filled with Him. We're to extend God's peace to *everyone*—in our families, the workplace, those inside and outside the church, the sales clerk who gives us extra help, as well as the "idiot" who cuts us off on the highway.

Seek God's Righteousness and Justice
Jesus tells us to *"Seek the Kingdom of God above all else, and live righteously . . ."* [3] God's Word holds the keys to "right living" and as Christians we should make it our priority to live by His standards in everything we do. Hebraic culture deeply connected righteousness, justice, and peace. Isaiah prophesied that Jesus, the Prince of Peace, would rule forever with *"fairness and justice."* [4] Similarly, Jeremiah 9:24 states, " . . . *I am the LORD who demonstrates unfailing love and who brings justice and righteousness to the earth . . . "*

This prophecy will be fulfilled at the Lord's second coming when a new heaven and earth are established where He will reign as King of kings and Lord of lords. Until that time, substantial injustice in the world remains. Someone once said, "In the end, everyone's dirty wash will be on display, and what a load of laundry there will be!" God will be the final judge of all humanity's actions.

Over the years, doing justice in the world has been the cause of considerable conflict among Christians. Should Christians be involved in war or not? Is it wrong for a Christian to work for a company that makes violent video games? These, and similar issues have been debated for years. Currently some focus all their attention on fighting for the unborn, while others say racial injustice is more important. Some Christians rally around causes to boycott stores that support gay marriage, or don't use the word "Christmas." While many of these issues get complex and may not have well-defined answers, one thing is clear—Scripture calls us to make peace in every facet of life.

Get Busy Serving

There are plenty of efforts we can support to bring peace to people that are clearly biblical—such as feeding the hungry, building homes for those who have suffered loss or can't afford one, sponsoring children to attend school in Africa, or sending care packages to the poor. We can volunteer to serve meals at soup kitchens, work at crisis pregnancy centers, visit and pray for those in hospitals, or lead Bible studies in nursing homes or prisons. It's important that we invest our lives in doing things that God favors, rather than spend countless hours just debating the difficult issues and doing nothing tangible.

Luke 4:18 makes our mission clear:

The Spirit of the LORD is upon me, for he has anointed me to bring Good News to the poor. He has sent me to proclaim that captives will be released, that the blind will see, that the oppressed will be set free.

Peacemakers treat all people with dignity and respect, including the most helpless and defenseless. Jesus says that when we feed the poor, offer hospitality to strangers, take care of the sick, and visit those in prison, it is like we are doing it to *Him*.

Then these righteous ones will reply, "Lord, when did we ever see you hungry and feed you? Or thirsty and give you something to drink? Or a stranger and show you hospitality? Or naked and give you clothing? When did we ever see you sick or in prison and visit you?" And the King will say, "I tell you the truth, when you did it to one of the least of these my brothers and sisters, you were doing it to me!" (Matthew 25:37-40)

Think about it! Jesus' words remind us of how much He values the service, love—and peace—we show to people around us.

The Peace That Lies Ahead

Living as peacemakers may often go against the cultural grain. It requires radical discipleship to follow Christ's commands to reach out to a lost and dying world. But each day that we walk in His love and speak His truth, we are one day closer to the time when all the world will truly be at peace—the way God originally intended. There's a day coming when God's peace will fill all the earth . . .

> *In the last days, the mountain of the LORD's house will be the highest of all—the most important place on earth. It will be raised above the other hills, and people from all over the world will stream there to worship. People from many nations will come and say, "Come, let us go up to the mountain of the LORD, to the house of Jacob's God. There he will teach us his ways, and we will walk in his paths." For the LORD's teaching will go out from Zion; his word will go out from Jerusalem. The LORD will mediate between nations and will settle international disputes. They will hammer their swords into plowshares and their spears into pruning hooks. Nation will no longer fight against nation, nor train for war anymore. (Isaiah 2:2-4)*

God gave the prophet Isaiah this vision of peace that will pervade the world in the age to come, when Jesus Christ will rule the earth. Weapons of warfare will be turned into farming implements and silos for nuclear missiles into grain silos. Nation will no longer fight against nation. There will be no more war.

God's creation will again be restored to paradise, as He originally intended. Intimate fellowship with our Creator, lost in the Fall and regained at the cross, will be fully reestablished. Fellowship with one another will be perfected and refreshed continually in the river of His perfect peace. Sorrow will be no more,[5] and in its place fullness of joy.

Today we experience God's peace, but not the fullness of peace. We enjoy Christ's presence, but only in part. In a world filled with brokenness and despair, and with sin continually nipping at our heels, God's promise of the peace that lies ahead strengthens us to move forward, to keep trusting and living for Him.

A Taste of What's to Come—Today

Every time God's peace enters our lives today we get a preview of the greater peace that will someday fill the earth. As we each walk out as peacemakers in our homes, churches, and the world around us, many will be blessed by our peacefulness. The glimpses of peace we experience today motivate us and others to seek less of ourselves, and more of Him.

- When a husband or wife chooses forgiveness over bitterness, we witness a preview of paradise.
- When a church group travels to a hurricane-ravaged area to rebuild homes for families in need, we get a glimpse of the glory that lies ahead.
- When the drug addict finds deliverance in Christ, we detect the dawning of that great day coming.
- When Christians open their homes to strangers in need, we view a hint of heavenly hospitality.
- When we donate food to feed the poor, we taste of the Messianic banquet ahead.
- When we give diapers and baby clothes to the local pregnancy center, we see a sign of the joy that's to come.
- When we help the widow with home repairs, we peek through a window to eternity.
- When we visit a hospital and pray for the sick, it's an indication of a better day ahead.

- When people whose lives have been imprisoned by brokenness and abuse discover wholeness in Jesus Christ, we find a foretaste of the future.

Each time we choose forgiveness over fault-finding, love over loathing, service over self . . . we embrace a hint of heaven. The promise of the fullness of peace that lies ahead joins us together with other Christians in a glorious fellowship of hope.

I pray that **God,** *the source of hope,* **will fill you completely with** *joy and* **peace because you trust in him.** *Then you will overflow with confident hope through the power of the Holy Spirit. (Romans 15:13)*

Eternity is on the horizon, but the dawn lingers. There is much work to be done.

We must be intentional about spending time with the Master daily. Meditate on His Word. Hide it in your heart. Bring Him all your praise, petitions and prayers. Meet Him in the secret place and find rest in His presence. Receive His fresh revelation words for you today.

> *With His perfect peace guarding our hearts, we will do less, but accomplish far more.*

When we feel life is too busy, it's easy to end up working by our own strength—until it runs dry. The world's frenetic pace leaves little room for peace. Yet the reality is that the busier we are, the more essential it is to be still in our hearts. Only then do we learn to hear the Shepherd's voice. With His perfect peace guarding our hearts, we will do less, but accomplish far more.

We'll be sharing the yoke with the Master—as He desires—allowing Him to lighten our load.

May you find rest and refreshment daily in the Prince of Peace, our Lord Jesus Christ. May His perfect peace dwell in you richly . . . as you carry His peace to a lost and dying world.

Jesus I am Resting, Resting

In 1865 J. Hudson Taylor formed the China Inland Mission, to bring the Word of God to China. In time, the work got the best of him. Overwhelmed with worry and work and nearing a breakdown, he found respite in a letter that came one day from fellow missionary, John McCarthy. In it, was the reminder from John 15 that our faith is strengthened not by struggling, but by abiding and resting in Jesus Christ.

"Jesus I am Resting, Resting"[6] later became Taylor's favorite hymn. Often, while taking a break from his busy schedule, he would sit at his organ and sing this hymn.

In closing, let us offer the words of this beautiful hymn to the Lord as our prayer:

Jesus I am resting, resting
In the Joy of what Thou art;
I am finding out the greatness
Of Thy loving heart.
Thou hast bid me gaze upon Thee,
And Thy beauty fills my soul,
For by Thy transforming power
Thou hast made me whole.

Peacemakers in a Troubled World

Jesus, I am resting, resting
In the joy of what Thou art;
I am finding out the greatness
Of Thy loving heart.

O how great Thy loving kindness,
Vaster, broader than the sea;
O how marvelous Thy goodness,
Lavished all on me.
Yes, I rest in Thee, Beloved,
Know what wealth of grace is Thine,
Know Thy certainty of promise,
And have made it mine.

Simply trusting Thee, Lord Jesus,
I behold Thee as Thou art;
And Thy love, so pure, so changeless,
Satisfies my heart.
Satisfies its deepest longings,
Meets, supplies its every need,
Compasseth me round with blessings,
Thine is love indeed!

Ever lift Thy face upon me,
As I work and wait for Thee;
Resting 'neath Thy smile, Lord Jesus,
Earth's dark shadows flee.
Brightness of my Father's glory,
Sunshine of my Father's face,
Keep me ever trusting, resting;
Fill me with Thy grace.

Endnotes

Author's Note
[1] Mark 11:24.

Part One—The Highest Perfection
[1] Soren Kierkegaard (1813-1855) was a Danish philosopher, theologian, poet, and Christian author.

Chapter 1—Our Deepest Need
[1] WebMD, "The Effects of Stress of Your Body", http://www.webmd.com/mental-health/effects-of-stress-on-your-body. Information based on a report from the U.S. Occupational Safety and Health Administration (OSHA).

[2] Ecclesiastes 1:9.

[3] Genesis 3.

[4] Colossians 1:21.

[5] Ephesians 2:1-10.

[6] Romans 6:22-23.

[7] Augustine of Hippo (354-430 A.D.), was an early Christian theologian whose writings are considered very influential in the development of western Christianity. The quote is from his work "The Confessions of Saint Augustine."

Chapter 2—The Many Faces of Peace

[1] OxfordDictionaries.com.

[2] Rick Renner, *Sparkling Gems from the Greek*, (Teach All Nations, 2007.)

[3] Luke 1:80, 2:52.

[4] Hebrews 13:5b (NKJV).

[5] Proverbs 8:17b (NKJV).

Chapter 3—Are You a Hebrew or a Greek?

[1] Abraham Heschel, *God in Search of Man*, (Farrar, Straus and Giroux; Reprint edition 1976), p. 34.

Chapter 4—Wisdom From Forrest

[1] The 1994 movie *Forrest Gump*, starring Tom Hanks won six Academy Awards and remains one of the highest grossing films of all time.

[2] Matthew 7:16a.

[3] John 14:21,23.

[4] Charles Swindoll, *Living Above the Level of Mediocrity: A Commitment to Excellence,* (Nashville, Tennessee: W Publishing Group, 1989), p. 242.

[5] "Word of life" is used in Philippians 2:16 and 1 John 1:1.

Endnotes

Part Two—10 Ways Jesus Can Give You Peace
[1] James Russell Miller (1840-1912) was a popular American Christian author and pastor.

Chapter 5—Yoked With the Master
[1] *The New Strong's Exhaustive Concordance of the Bible*, by James Strong, (Thomas Nelson Publishers 2010), usage 3875.

[2] The Greek reads "grace upon grace."

Chapter 6—A Prayer-Full Life
[1] Roger Steer, *George Muller: Delighted in God*, (Harold Shaw Publishers, revised edition 1981), p. 226-227.

[2] George Muller (1805-1898).

[3] Frances de Sales (1567-1622) was the Bishop of Geneva.

[4] John 14:26.

[5] Charles L. Allen, *All Things Are Possible Through Prayer*, (Revell 2003), p. 85-86. Dale Carnegie (1888-1955) was an American writer, lecturer, and the developer of famous courses in self-improvement, salesmanship, public speaking, and interpersonal skills. His bestselling books *How to Win Friends and Influence People* (1936), and *How to Stop Worrying and Start Living* (1948), remain popular today.

[6] Sarì Harrar and Rita DeMaria, Reader's Digest, "Advice for Long-Married Couples,"
http://www.rd.com/advice/relationships/intimacy-in-the-

golden-years-of-marriage/.

[7] Frank C. Laubach (1884-1970) was known as "The Apostle to the Illiterates." In 1935, he developed the "Each One Teach One" literacy program while working in the Philippines. It has been used to teach about 60 million people to read in their own language. He was deeply concerned about poverty, injustice and illiteracy, and considered them barriers to peace in the world.

[8] R.A. Torrey (1856-1928) was an American evangelist, pastor, educator and writer.

Chapter 7—Heading East, Heading West
[1] Ron Lee Davis, *A Forgiving God in an Unforgiving World*, (Harvest House Publishers 1984), p. 26.

[2] See also Hebrews 10:17 and Jeremiah 31:34.

[3] Kurt E. Koch, *Occult Bondage and Deliverance,* (Kregel Publications 1972), p. 10.

Chapter 8—Letting Go of the Rope
[1] William Barclay, *The Letter to the Hebrews*, (Westminster John Knox Press 2002), p. 128-129. Barclay (1907-1978) was a Scottish minister, author, and radio and television presenter.

[2] See 2 Corinthians 2:5-11 and Ephesians 4:26-27.

[3] Cornelia ("Corrie") ten Boom (1892-1983).

[4] Craig Brian Larson, *750 Engaging Illustrations for Preachers,*

Teachers, and Writers, (Baker Books 2007), p. 224.

Chapter 9—A Royal Wardrobe
[1] John 10:10.

[2] Jesus Christ, the Living Word, is truth. See John 14:6, John 1:17 (NKJV), Ephesians 4:21.

[3] While many believe the *"sword of the Spirit which is the **word of God**"* in Ephesians 6:17 is referring to the Bible and the power of putting Scriptures in our minds, it's actually much more than that. The Greek for "word" used here is *rhema* (Strong's 4487)—the conversational "word" of the Spirit. It's the Lord's speaking to us a revelation word specific to our circumstance. This tremendous working of the Spirit in us assures us of the victory we have in Him to reign in life.

Chapter 10—Growing Giant Pumpkins
[1] Thad Starr, "How To Grow A Giant Pumpkin," http://www.starrfarms.net/Howtogrowagiant.htm.

[2] Read the full record of the sower and the seed in Luke 8:4-15.

[3] "Word" in Luke 8 is the Greek word *logos* (Strong's 3056)—referring to God's overarching plan or purpose for life and the universe, as set forth in the Bible.

[4] See also Matthew 13:23.

[5] See Matthew 12:33 and Luke 3:8-9 for similar records.

---

[6] In Galatians 5:22 "fruit" is the Greek word *karpós* (Strong's 2590), which is in the singular. The same word is used in John 15 for "fruit." It implies that everything is done in true partnership with Christ, i.e. a believer (a branch) lives in union with Christ (the Vine). By definition, *karpós* results from *two* life-streams— the Lord living His life through ours—to yield what is eternal (see 1 John 4:17).

[7] See Galatians 5:6. "Expressing" is the Greek word *energéō* (Strong's 1754) from 1722 /*en*, "engaged in," which intensifies 2041 /*érgon*, "work"—which means to energize, or working in a situation which brings it from one stage or point to the next, like an electrical current energizing a wire, bringing it to a shining light bulb. In light of this definition, we see that our faith is energized by love.

Chapter 11—Saved to Serve

[1] John Kenneth Galbraith, *A Life in Our Times*, (Houghton Mifflin 1981), p. 121. Galbraith (1908-2006), was a Canadian-American economist, public official, and diplomat.

[2] See Chapter 5 for a detailed explanation of a "yoke."

[3] 2 Corinthians 5:21.

[4] Mother Teresa (1910-1997) was a Roman Catholic nun, known for her missionary work to the poor around the world.

[5] Rick Warren, *Daily Hope*, November 16, 2010, www.purposedriven.com.

[6] Ibid., June 28, 2010.

⁷ *Doule* is the feminine form of the Greek term *doulos.*

⁸ Romans 1:1.

⁹ Luke 1:38 (NKJV). *Rhema* is used in this verse for "word."

¹⁰ Andrew Murray (1828-1917) was a South African pastor, writer, and teacher.

¹¹ Ephesians 4:29 (NKJV).

¹² Ecclesiastes 11:4 TLB.

Chapter 12—The Miraculous Mind of Christ
¹ Story first reported in The Deseret News, September 9, 1988, "Brain-tissue Transplant Results in Chickens that Sound Like Quails."

² Strong's 1492.

³ Strong's 1097.

⁴ 1 Corinthians 13:12a.

⁵ See also Matthew 6:24.

Chapter 13—Daily Transformation
¹ Strong's 3339.

² *The New World Dictionary* defines metamorphosis as "a complete change of physical form or substance," or "the rapid

transformation of a larva into an adult that occurs in certain animals; for example the stage between tadpole and frog or between chrysalis and butterfly." (www.dictionary.com)

3 Information gathered from: Dr. Lincoln Brower, "Inside the Chrysalis," Monarch Butterfly Journey North, www.learner.org. Also, "Be Ye Transformed," Christian Life and Doctrine, June 1999, www.dawnbible.com.

4 Colossians 1:27b.

5 Strong's 3345.

6 *Vine's Expository Dictionary of Old & New Testament Words,* (Thomas Nelson 2003).

7 2 Corinthians 11:13-15: *"These people are false apostles. They are deceitful workers who **disguise** themselves as apostles of Christ. But I am not surprised! Even Satan **disguises** himself as an angel of light. So it is no wonder that his servants also **disguise** themselves as servants of righteousness. In the end they will get the punishment their wicked deeds deserve."*

8 Philippians 4:13.

Chapter 14—Internalizing Truth
1 Sam Freney, "The Benefits of Memorizing Scripture," September 10, 2012, mathiasmedia.com/briefing. Also, Zara Dawtrey, "A NZ Death Shocks Grammar," The Examiner, January 24, 2011, www.examiner.com.au.

[2] Charles Swindoll, *Growing Strong in the Seasons of Life*, (Grand Rapids: Zondervan, 1994), p. 61.

[3] Danielle Marois, "The Benefits of Memorizing Scripture," July 26, 2012, www.examiner.com.

[4] Ann Voskamp, "Your Care Guide: 25 Point Manifesto for Sanity in 2013," *A Holy Experience* blog, www.aholyexperience.com.

[5] Current websites as of the writing of this book are: memverse.com, scripturetyper.com, quizlet.com, qstream.com.

[6] An app is a computer software program or application. Mobile apps are designed to run on smartphones, tablet computers, and other mobile devices.

[7] Reader's Digest, August 1981.

[8] "Meditation," http://en.wikipedia.org/wiki/Meditation.

[9] Joyce Huggett, *Learning the Language of Prayer*, (Crossroad Publishing Company, New York, 1997), p. 38. Huggett is one of England's bestselling Christian authors, and was previously a missionary to Cyprus.

[10] John 16:13.

[11] Bruce Demarest, *Satisfy Your Soul*, (NavPress Publishing Group, 1999), p. 133.

[12] Psalm 1:2; Joshua 1:8.

Part Three—Living in the Lord's Presence
[1] Sheila Walsh (1956-present) is a Scottish-born contemporary Christian vocalist, author, Bible teacher, and inspirational speaker.

Chapter 15—Peace Under Pressure
[1] Norman Lee Macht, *Connie Mack: The Turbulent and Triumphant Years, 1915-1931*, (University of Nebraska Press), p. 195.

[2] Strong's 3309. Other interesting uses of *merimnao* are found in Luke 10:41; 12:11, 12, 22, 25 and 26; 1 Corinthians 7:32-34; 12:25; Philippians 2:20.

[3] 1 Peter 5:7. Here, the noun form *merimna* (Strong's 3308) is used instead of *merimnao*.

[4] Philippians 4:7 (KJV).

[5] 2 Timothy 1:7.

[6] 1 John 4:18.

[7] Dr. E. Stanley Jones, *Transformed by Thorns*, p. 95. (Out of print). Jones (1884-1973), was a Methodist missionary and theologian.

[8] Ephesians 4:27 (NKJV).

[9] 2 Peter 3:9b.

[10] John 16:33.

[11] In 2 Corinthians 4:17-18 "present troubles" is the Greek word *thlipsis* (Strong's 2347): meaning persecution, affliction, distress, or tribulation. It literally means "*pressure* (what constricts or rubs together), used of a narrow place that 'hems someone in'; ... especially *internal pressure* that causes someone to feel confined, restricted, or without options."

[12] 2 Corinthians 4:17-18 (NKJV) uses "light affliction" instead of "present trouble" (NLT).

[13] Luke 23:34a.

Chapter 16—The Quiet Classroom
[1] Pythagoras of Samos (570-495 B.C.).

[2] Blaise Pascal (1623-1662).

[3] Robert Murray McCheyne (1813-1843).

[4] Robert Murray McCheyne, *The Works of Rev. Robert Murray McCheyne: Complete in One Volume*, p. 140-141.

[5] E.M. Bounds (1835-1913).

[6] E. M. Bounds, *Power through Prayer* (1906), available at Christian Classics Etheral Library Website, http://www.ccel.org/ccel/bounds/power.IX.html

[7] George Muller, *Autobiography of George Muller*, (Nisbet & Co., London, 1906), p. 152-153.

[8] George Muller, *The Autobiography of George Muller*, (Whitaker House, 1984), p. 117-119.

[9] With smartphones and tablet computers.

[10] 1 Timothy 6:17.

[11] 1 Kings 19:12.

[12] This concept is from: Sarah Young, *Jesus Calling*, (Thomas Nelson, Inc. 2004), October 30 entry, p. 317.

[13] Francis de Sales (1567-1622) was Bishop of Geneva and is honored as a saint in the Roman Catholic Church. He's noted for his deep faith and gentle approach to the religious divisions resulting from the Protestant Reformation. He's also known for his writings on spiritual formation, particularly *Introduction to the Devout Life* and *Treatise on the Love of God*.

[14] Written in 1882 by William D. Longstaff.

Chapter 17—My Sheep Hear My Voice
[1] Lee Dye, "Babies Recognize Mom's Voice From the Womb," Technology News, May 23, 2013. ABCnews.go.com.

[2] Tina Ghose, Staff Writer, "Who's Got Better Baby Sense: Mom or Dad?", LiveScience, April 16, 2013, www.livescience.com.

[3] John 20:11-18.

[4] Genesis 3.

⁵ Romans 1:20.

⁶ Not exhaustive lists.

⁷ Strong's 4487.

⁸ 1 Kings 19:12.

⁹ Ezekiel 20:37 (NKJV).

¹⁰ Matthew 11:28. See also Chapter 5—"Yoked With The Master."

Chapter 18—Your Best State of Mind

¹ Amit Amin, "The Science of Gratitude: More Benefits Than Expected—26 Studies and Counting" and "The 31 Benefits of Gratitude You Didn't Know About: How Gratitude Can Change Your Life," www.happierhuman.com.

² Bob Burg, "Giving Thanks—A Post-Thanksgiving Thought," Early to Rise, December 6, 2013. www.earlytorise.com.

³ Psalm 100:4.

⁴ Luke 6:20-23.

⁵ Numbers 11:13.

⁶ Exodus 17:1-6.

⁷ Numbers 11:1.

---

[8] Matthew 10:30.

[9] Merlin Carothers, *Prison to Praise*, (1970), p. 91-92. This book had its 97th printing in 2010. It's been translated into 58 languages and has sold millions of copies. *Prison to Praise* has changed the lives of countless Christians as they learn they can "live in peace as they discover the secrets of a life of praise."

[10] Nehemiah 8:10.

Chapter 19—Peacemakers in a Troubled World
[1] Donald Kraybill, Steven Nolt, and David Weaver-Zercher, *Amish Grace: How Forgiveness Transcended Tragedy,* (San Francisco: John Wiley & Sons, 2007). This powerful story is retold in this book.

[2] These directives are outlined in Matthew 18:15-20.

[3] Matthew 6:33.

[4] Isaiah 9:6-7.

[5] Revelation 21:1-4.

[6] Jean Sopia Pigott wrote the poem "Jesus I am Resting, Resting" in 1876. That same year James Mountain wrote music to it. It has long been known as one of the most beloved and revered hymns of all time. Thomas Wellesley Pigott, Jean's brother and a missionary in China, was martyred during the Boxer Rebellion.

You will keep in perfect peace
all who trust in you,
all whose thoughts are fixed on you!
Isaiah 26:3